My Life Remembered

*"I am a Yankee, the second child in a sea of brothers,
and have a natural bent toward revolution and reform."*

Also by Rachel Hosmer

Gender and God

RACHEL HOSMER

My Life Remembered

NUN ✳ PRIEST ✳ FEMINIST

COWLEY PUBLICATIONS
Cambridge ✦ Boston
Massachusetts

Published in the United States of America by Cowley Publications, a division of the Society of St. John the Evangelist. No portion of this book may be reproduced, stored in or introduced into a retrieval system, or transmitted, in any form or by any means—including photocopying—without the prior written permission of Cowley Publications, except in the case of brief quotations embodied in critical articles and reviews.

International Standard Book Number: 1-56101-044-8

Library of Congress Number: 91-27686

Library of Congress Cataloging-in-Publication Data

Hosmer, Rachel.

My life remembered : nun, priest, feminist / Rachel Hosmer : Joyce Glover, editor.

p. cm.

ISBN 1-56101-044-8 (alk. paper) : $11.95

1. Hosmer, Rachel. 2. Episcopal Church—Clergy—Biography. 3. Anglican Communion—Clergy—Biography. 4. Women clergy—United States—Biography. 5. Clergy—United States—Biography.

I. Glover, Joyce. II. Title.

BX5995.H69A3 1991

283'.092—dc20   91-27686

This book is printed on acid-free paper and was produced in the United States of America.

Cowley Publications
28 Temple Place
Boston, Massachusetts 02111

Editor's Preface

Rachel Hosmer had been my spiritual director for about seven years when I began working with her on her memoirs in the spring of 1988. At that time, she was undergoing chemotherapy, with its accompanying bouts of nausea and exhaustion. On what she called her "good days" Rachel, in her determination to finish the book, taped new material and read and revised already completed chapters. Frequently in our times together, Rachel acknowledged her inability to recall fully and accurately the details of various experiences and emphasized the need for her editors to flesh out her account with details that eluded her at that time.

Rachel died in late December 1988, soon after Cowley Publications had accepted the manuscript. As Cynthia Shattuck and I scrutinized the manuscript closely, we decided to seek help from a number of people close to Rachel, particularly those who had corresponded with her, in order to fill in the gaps in her account. I would like to thank especially Tilden Edwards and Charlotte Moore, who supplied portions of their correspondence with Rachel that helped to give a more rounded portrait; Mary Coelho, who talked with me about the years she worked closely with Rachel at General Theological Seminary; and Patricia Wilson-Kastner, Rachel's literary executor. Nan Mein, who gave me some helpful comments on the chapter on Bolahun, and Florence Mepham, who provided important details concerning the Oxford Conferences, also deserve special thanks.

I would also like to thank members of Rachel's community, the Order of St. Helena, for permission to use their archives and to quote from the group memoir *Early Days,* which tells of the founding of the order. Sister Cornelia, Superior, Sister Jean Campbell, Sister Josephine, and Sister Mary Michael Simpson have all read the manuscript at various stages and made many helpful suggestions.

The reader will notice from time to time small italicized excerpts either from Rachel's letters or from *Early Days,* to which Rachel contributed a chapter. We have used them in places where it seemed important to supply additional details or to elucidate a situation that seems unclear. We believe that the excerpts from Rachel's letters are particularly powerful in bringing her before us in all her forcefulness, her curiosity, her humor, and her wisdom.

Joyce Glover

Table of Contents

Foreword

*I*n September of 1982 I began teaching at the General Theological Seminary. During that first fall, early on an October afternoon, I found myself in our first floor apartment, deep in a friendly conversation with a veteran colleague. The Rev. Sr. Rachel Hosmer, O.S.H. had come to welcome me, discuss the general state of the seminary, particularly the role of women, and to garner some advice from me about one of the pressing campus issues of that month. How characteristic that she would not wait, but came to me. And what vintage Rachel that she choose to test me, not by garnering information, but by eliciting insights and vision.

Before she walked into the apartment, I knew she would prove to be a strong and remarkable person. She was a religious and a priest; a common combination for males but most rare among women. She had been one of the founding members of her community, and been a strong if sometimes controversial voice among Episcopal religious. In the seventies, she was the first ordained woman to be a full-time member of General's faculty. Faculty and students alike had told me much about her intelligence, compassion, fearsome conscience, concern for peace and justice issues, and her gentle but astonishing capacity to grasp the depths of another's character. By the end of the hour, I knew I had found a friend.

Over the next six years we spent much valuable time together. I count myself fortunate to have been one of these privileged to know Rachel and walk with her during those last years when she shared freely the wisdom of a long and remarkable lifetime. One of Rachel's most amazing characteristics was her capacity to appreciate and draw the best from a wide range of people from various ages and backgrounds. Her vision and achievements owe much of their richness to the ecumenical composition of that, literally, world-wide group who counted themselves "one of Rachel's friends." Her heart and mind had grown wide and deep from her beginnings in Everett, Massachusetts in 1908.

This autobiography, carefully edited and supplemented by her friend Joyce Glover, is, as she tells us, a legacy. It was written during the last months of her life, as she lay "dying and healing, at the same time." As the cancer coursed all too quickly through her frail body, she spent herself in writing what she intended as a gift of love for her sisters in the Order of St. Helena, and the wider community of the Church catholic. It was, as she noted with a familiar gleam in her eye, "a life remembered," not necessarily "what really happened."

Everyone who knew Rachel well will be delighted with so much fascinating insight into her life, and all the great causes of the day with which she was so involved. But she has also deliberately omitted much of importance to her and to those causes. For example, she is very vague about some of the circumstances surrounding the foundation of the Order of St. Helena, because she felt that to be more specific about some of the people or situations might hurt those who still remember them. Thus, her comments are very restrained and sparse. Although some may wish she had been more forthcoming, we see the value of her reticence when we note the pain and distress caused by today's "tell all" biographies and memoirs which seem designed to titillate the reader and hurt the people described. Rachel's silence is never intended to deceive, but she purposefully avoided comments or evaluations which might appear to harm another's reputation.

She did not intend to give an exact account of everything she did or taught, but looking back from her deathbed, to sift what she perceived as the important from the insignificant, the worthy and edifying from the hurtful and distressing, and to give us a portrait of the Rachel she wanted us to remember. Even if we would have chosen differently, she offers us a true self from these pages. She speaks with a voice shaped by a rectitude rooted in generations of New Englanders, the world-embracing compassion of Unitarian religious sentiment at its best, the discipline of Catholic monastic life in its passionate search for God, and the emerging vision of contemporary feminism with its new hopes and expectations for humanity.

As we see her life take shape through these pages, we each are given a precious gift. Her sisters in the Order of St. Helena receive new insight into their own beginnings, and into the heart and mind of one whose life is inextricably bound up with the community's character. Anglican and other religious gain a valued testimony to the development of a leader who spanned the twentieth-century change in monasticism from medieval (or pseudo-medieval) to present day forms of the religious life. Christian feminists discover the witness of a pioneer priest and religious woman, with a constantly growing and developing consciousness, one that grew naturally from her efforts to find and proclaim God in the contemporary world. All of us are challenged by her life struggle to offer herself wholeheartedly to God, to share in the vibrant power of God's life, through which she was able to empower others. Her prayerful communion with God breathed life into everything she was and did.

> O lux beatissima,
> Reple cordis intima
> tuorum fidelium.

Patricia Wilson-Kastner

My Beginnings

And now that I am old and gray-headed, O God,
do not forsake me,
till I make known your strength
to this generation
and your power to all who are to come. (Ps. 71:18)

I am lying here in bed on the first floor of the Manhattan convent, recovering from an operation for cancer. The cat is on top of me—she thinks she owns the bed! I have a beautiful view out the back door into the garden, and the Sisters here are taking the most beautiful, loyal, loving care of me that can be imagined. My illness has given me a chance to get together this account of my life and my vocation. It is going to be written simply, for I have not the strength or agility for research. Instead, I am calling upon my memory. This means that the account is subjective, not objective. Because my life seems to be coming to an end, I want to leave a record.

I was born in Massachusetts in 1908, in Everett, on Hosmer Street, into a New England family, inheriting from both sides the tradition of stalwart dissent and independence, and from my mother's side a certain rambunctiousness. My mother's people were seafarers. Her grandfather was a sea captain, married to the daughter of another sea captain. My grandmother, as a child, had been taken on voyages around the Horn, all the way to China. I loved to talk with her about it. She knew a great deal about seafaring subjects. We used to say, "Grandma, talk nautical!" She did not like to do it very much, because there was a sharp distinction between the captain's daughter and the crew in her day. They talked nautical, however, and she overheard it, so she could talk nautical if she wanted to. She used to slip off from her mother's watchful care sometimes and secretly get the crew to help her with her daily stint of sewing on a patchwork quilt that every properly brought up child was required to do. Besides telling us stories, she taught us how to box the compass and how to name the sails on a clipper ship, from the flying jib to the crojack and spanker. I remember one day when my brother John came home from school with a little drawing of what he called a ship. Grandmother looked at it and said scornfully, "Looks like a dish of ice cream!"

Although Grandmother did not live with us, we saw a good deal of her. She was an important person for me. Most of all, she was an image of courage. She had had polio as a small child and was taken to Liverpool for mud baths, but of course that was of very little help. When I knew her, she would fill the tub up every morning with cold water and splash around in it like a grampus as a way of dealing with the effects of polio. She also used to wear long, red flannel bandages on her great deformed hip. One of the things that I learned as a child is that you are never to make fun of people over things they cannot help. I think this was rooted in our sensitivity to Grandmother, for we loved her dearly. She was kind and fair. She never told on us. If we did something that displeased her, she would get after us, but she did not tell tales on us. And she loved us.

My father's side was also of New England heritage, all the way back to about 1640. Some of my Hosmer forebears were Unitarian divines, some of them were Yankee merchants, and some of them, I suppose, were farmers. They were involved in the Revolution. The officer who gave the command to fire the first shot at Lexington was named Hosmer, I have been told. My father was a self-made man who only finished the twelfth grade. His parents had very little to help him with. They were not rich, but they were proper people, correct people, who had inherited a family tradition of their own. The street I was born on was named after Old Deacon Hosmer, a Baptist preacher, but even so, they were not big, important people. My father was the youngest of three children, and I think much the most adventurous of his family and also a very capable man. He built up a good business of his own—a wholesale flour business—by intelligence, hard work, honesty, and by many hidden, simple, good things that he did for people along the way, things we learned of mostly after his death.

I inherit from both sides a strength, a rootedness in New England soil, a sense of independence, curiosity, a love of adventure, a desire to enjoy life without fearing it and a deep respect for the truth. Neither one of my parents had any use for lying. I remember being at a meeting somewhere or other, and the question was asked, "What do you remember about the first time your parents lied to you?" And the only reply I came up with was, "They never did." They were straight with us.

Ours was a strong family. My mother and my father worked together in bringing my brothers and me up. (I have one older brother and two younger ones, so I lived with a male majority.) Neither parent ran the house alone; they talked things over. They did not argue about our behavior or our need of discipline in front of us. I knew they fought; I knew they were unhappy sometimes, but their struggles were not carried out in our presence. One dreadful time the light of the world went out for me. They had had a row, and my mother came downstairs and went out. I could tell she was angry. She was away for hours and hours, and I was afraid she was never coming back. It was total abandonment. I went upstairs to a clothes closet where an evening coat of hers was hanging. I can see it yet—watered silk, blue and green, with an ecru-colored lace collar. I sat there crying into it. She did come back that night and was very distressed to realize that I had not known she was coming back. She said, "I told you I would come back." This memory of mine speaks of my first experience of abandonment, but it is also a symbol of my mother's centrality in the family.

Nobody in our family could put down a woman for being inferior because my mother was so clearly the hearth fire of that family. She saw to our comfort, that we had proper clothing, that our shoes were big enough, that we had three good, solid New England meals every day—I never had a poor meal in my mother's house. My mother was absolutely dependable. She was not bossy; she was honest and fair and direct. Some things she would not put up with, like dirty stories, for instance. She was very impatient with parents who frightened their children and prevented them from exploring and finding out things for themselves.

As we grew up, we were allowed that freedom. We learned to ride and to ski and to swim. I was allowed to go alone up to the lake to swim with my friends. When I was about eight or ten, I swam across the lake and came back in great triumph. It took a while for my family to believe it!

When my parents did interesting things with their friends, they would include us. I remember a little shack in the woods and a group of my parents' friends that went snowshoeing out to it. My parents gave me a pair of snowshoes just the right size so that I could go along too. When we got out there, we made a big fire and fried chocolate doughnuts, then snowshoed home again. Such things were just part of my whole experience.

My father took us every year as a family to Newfoundland to fish for salmon. He arranged the trips, something he did very well. We went by ship from Boston to Yarmouth, took a train through Nova Scotia to North Sydney, then another little boat across to Port aux Basques. There we took a strange old train with oil lamps swinging from the ceiling, up the west side of Newfoundland to our camp on the Corduroy River where we spent two or three wonderful weeks salmon fishing. We went comfortably by train and by ship. When we got to our destination, we were met by a crew of guides who took us downstream to the camp. Just as he had with the snowshoes, my father equipped me appropriately, this time with a light rod, strong enough to do its job—to catch a salmon—and easy enough for me to handle. I learned from him how to cast, how to play a fish, how to bring it in. He was an expert sportsman, and those things he liked to do, he did very well indeed. This was evident in the way he put out a salmon line, such a long line, just a few inches above the surface, then dropped it gently on the surface of the river. Out of his love for knowing all about whatever interested him, he learned how to make flies and all about the life of the salmon. An etching of a salmon leaping the falls to go upstream to spawn was a particular favorite of his, for he admired the courage and independence of that creature.

My father also loved the stars, and he shared his love and appreciation for nature with us. He taught us how to play tennis, another source of enjoyment for him, and continued to play it until he was no longer able to see. He was expert at chess and instructed us in that too. He could sit at the back of the living room at home, without seeing the board, while Dick, my younger brother, and I would take him on. Even though Dick and I could consult and look at the board, my father could beat us every time.

As I continue to think about my childhood memories, there comes to my mind my first experience of dread, an emotion not unconnected with cancer. It would have been in 1914 when I was six. I was sitting on the floor as I remember. My father came home from Boston with the *Boston Evening Transcript*, which was open as usual, but not to the financial news. He said to my mother in a voice loaded with dread such as I had never heard before, "Lottie, it looks as if there's going to be war in Europe." And I heard my mother say something like, "Cal, there couldn't possibly be, not in this day and age." I already knew from my family and from my grandmother that we lived in a country with oceans on either side and that beyond the oceans there were people—different people from us. I grew up with that idea, that perspective, in a family where public affairs were of interest, were talked about, and where my elders took their share of responsibility about voting, criticizing the outgoing governor, and so forth. So I felt part of a democracy from childhood.

World War I did break out, and the rising tide of anti-German attitudes showed itself both in school and in the playground. German poetry, German music—all were no good. Every German you saw in a cartoon was wearing a spiked helmet and carrying a dead baby, with the burning library of Louvain in the background. The Germans were beasts, and we were angels; Joan of Arc was coming to rescue the good from the bad.

My older brother reacted to America's eventual entry into the war in a way that I suppose was normal for a teenager of his day. He and his friend Tom Ironmonger got the bright idea of enlisting. Since they realized they would have to be over eighteen in order to be accepted, they took off their shoes and chalked an 18 on the soles so that they could say as they stood there, "Yes, I'm over 18!" They tried it out at the nearest local recruiting office. The man behind the desk took one look at them and said, "Go home and join the Boy Scouts!" They were greatly humiliated. Calvin tried to compensate for that by joining the National Guard. During the Boston Police strike, he had a great time riding about Boston on police horses as a volunteer strike-breaker. The military streak in my family is strong.

We bought Liberty Bonds, wore buttons and waved the flag. And in the end, suddenly there came the news of the

Armistice. The first news was false, but a few days later the real cease-fire took place. People ran out into the streets, ringing the bells and celebrating.

During World War I it was customary for families like ours to invite soldiers and sailors on leave in Boston from the war zone to come and share with us on the feast days—Thanksgiving Day, for instance. Little by little we got to know British seamen and British Army officers— two in particular—and to hear their point of view and a different way of looking at life. One time Calvin had a row with one of them about who had the best navy, Britain or the United States, and finally got Harry down on the floor and sat on top of him. When Harry protested, "Let me up," Calvin demanded, "Who's got the best navy?" Harry responded, "You have, you have, let me up!"

As I try to link some of this with my present life, I realize that dread is part of my awareness of other countries and cultures, of my concern for them, of my consciousness. As I write this on Palm Sunday, 1988, I am very conscious of the world situation in Israel, in South Africa, in Central America, in Liberia, in Ireland, in my own country. My prayers and my concern, my hopes and my fears, include all those people, my brothers and my sisters over the planet, everywhere.

I grew up in Sharon, a small town in Massachusetts, about twenty miles south of Boston. Many of the people on our street commuted to Boston every day on the train and came home at night bearing their copies of the *Boston Evening Transcript* and the steak or fresh fish for dinner. I played with other children on that street where I also went to school. Since both the grammar school and primary school were within a couple of blocks of our house, I could walk there as most children did in those days. I went to school in Sharon until I finished the eighth grade, and was sent to Boston to the Girls' Latin School on the Fenway.

I took a train every day, along with my brother and my father. The school pounded into my head a real understanding of the ancient world and the elements of English grammar. I could diagram any sentence that ever existed; I knew the proper name for every kind of figure of speech that ever was; I was good in history and English. When it came to math, I was just a dud. I wasted my time and my teacher's time by refusing to learn the binomial theorem. I had it in my head from my father that after a certain point everything you put into your head drove something else out. As a result, I got the idea very early that I must be careful about what I put into my head so that I would not lose the things that I liked! When it came to the requirement to learn the binomial theorem, I thought, "I'm never going to have any use for that."

When I arrived home every day from Girls' Latin School, do you think I sat down and did my homework? I did not! I would go out and saddle up the mare and take her out. We had a couple of riding horses and a pony, and my older brother Calvin taught us all how to ride and take care of an animal who serves you. He pointed out that "This is a strong, beautiful creature, but she will be afraid if you're not sure what you're doing. When you mount her, you take charge, because she expects you to keep her out of trouble. If you feel her getting frightened, put your hand on her neck and speak to her. When you bring her in, you walk her the last mile, take off her saddle, rub up the hide underneath the saddle where it's all sweaty. Give her a few drinks, but not too many, with water out of the bucket. Later on she can have more water and more food." It was a lesson I have never forgotten about our relationship to other creatures.

My childhood is full of memories of beautiful rides into the country, often alone, but usually with Jack, the family dog, who went everywhere with us. He was a beautiful mongrel, a mix of sheep dog and collie, who lived with, and among, the Hosmer family. Jack was not allowed on the beds, but he would sneak upstairs and I would let him get into bed with me. When he heard my mother's footsteps on the lowest step, he would slide out quietly. He was big and very friendly with everyone—a good companion. He went to church with us and to school; everyone knew him. He went daily to the butcher shop for his bone. One day when he went in, the bone he was given was too small so he put it down and barked at the butcher, who then gave him a bigger one!

Jack too was part of my experience, my interrelationship with other creatures. How valuable, how interesting, how amusing, and also what a responsibility he was! We were expected to take care of Jack. Whatever we did, he was right in the middle of it. When he went swimming with us, we would pull him up on the raft. He came home with us when we were ready. On a pony ride, he would get in the pony cart with us; when we went riding, he went along too. He was part of the family. All these are very happy, brightly colored, carefully treasured, detailed memories of childhood in Sharon, Massachusetts, back in the first decades of this century.

Our introduction to social life in Sharon began with dancing class. The girls sat on one side, the boys on the other. The dancing teacher had a little clicker she used when she wanted us to stop or start. We were taught how to respond to an invitation to dance. The little girls stood on one side and the little boys advanced in a wavering line towards us. Each boy stood in front of a girl, placed one hand upon his stomach and the other hand on his back, made a little bow and said, "May I please have the pleasure of the next dance?" The little girl gracefully accepted. We practiced this a time or two, and then we carried it out. We were taught the two-step, the waltz, and the foxtrot.

It was customary to carry your dancing slippers in a green bag, and one of the delights of dancing school was that whatever boy got to carry a girl's green bag often had to fight off other contenders. That was a great time for a girl. One night a boy hired another boy to beat up a third boy so boy number one could walk me home and carry the green bag. As I grew older, I went to country club dances and small parties in other people's houses and in my own house. At one dance my older brother became very protective of me when the boy I was dancing with lifted me off my feet. I saw my brother coming over with fire in his eye. He tapped my escort on the shoulder and said, "That's my sister. Don't do that again." So I was introduced into the society of a little New England town, which meant I learned early that the relation between the sexes was a good one, that it needed to be regulated, kept from excess, and that a certain amount of decorum was required. The joy of dancing was part of that. It is all related to the fact that because my family did not usually use sanctions to enforce behavior, I was spared some guilt feelings.

When I was about fourteen, I was thrown off a horse and received a painful shoulder injury. Except for aspirin, I did very little about it at that time. However, in time the injury necessitated trips to several doctors. The last one was Dr. Smith-Petersen in Boston. From that point on he was my friend and a trusted mentor. He was very shrewd, very loving and took charge of me in a firm way, trying to keep me from overdoing and straining. He cautioned me, "Your engine is too big for the chassis." All the time I was his patient, until his death, he insisted that I get regular rest and exercise.

I also wore a brace for a time. The accident seemed to have destabilized both my spine and shoulder in some way, so that for the rest of my life I have had a certain amount of back pain to contend with. One of my methods of dealing with it has been to say to myself, "Pain is a kind of consciousness. If I'm not too conscious of it, I'm not going to feel it." So I discouraged people from asking, "How is your back?" and kept myself from talking about it. Perhaps this attitude has spread over into other kinds of pain in my life. It has its good side, but its bad side as well. It has been important in helping me get through some things I have wanted to do when my body was not very strong. All of this has gone into the person that I am and my attitude towards asceticism and towards the body. I am aware of my own strength and my weakness as I try to cope today with the malignancy and the chemotherapy.

A very important legacy from my father to us was his respect for books. He never read trashy books but read both fully and voluminously in whatever interested him, often reading it aloud to us whether we had an interest in it or not! My mother came home one time after leaving him baby-sitting to find him droning away to us from *The Minor Tactics of Chess*! I am afraid we drowsed a bit. His taste in books ran to history—Lecky's *History of European Morals* and American history—seafaring books as well as books about whatever he was doing or was interested in at the time—like the life of the salmon. He gave us some respect for the book itself, for the way to treat a book, and got angry with us when we took books out of the library and did not get them back on time. My parents always gave us nice books at Christmas time, illustrated children's books like *Robin Hood* and *Knights of the Round Table*. My real favorite was *Treasure Island*, which I read six times over.

My older brother Calvin also contributed to our respect for and delight in reading. He loved fine editions, for one thing, and taught me how to handle a book carefully, and how to appreciate the way it was made. Calvin also taught me to love poetry, and it was he who read to me while I was quite small his favorite poem, "To a Water Fowl," by William Cullen Bryant.

> Whither, midst falling dew,
> While glow the heavens with the last steps of day,
> Far, through their rosy depths, dost thou pursue
> Thy solitary way
> He who, from zone to zone,

> Guides through the boundless sky thy certain flight,
> In the long way that I must tread alone,
> Will lead my steps aright.

Somehow the theme of that poem has stayed with me all my life!

There was no television in those days, and the radio was seldom used. At night we played games and read before the fire, or we popped corn, had friends in and played games, or rolled up the rugs and danced. Or we fenced and made a mess of all the rugs. We had a wonderful game that we played outside with the dog, who would chase us from porch to porch. We could jump the rails, but he would have to go around, and it was a loud, boisterous performance we all enjoyed. I do not know if my mother enjoyed it inside the house, but she never tried to stop us. That really was her way—there were many things she put up with, but when she was unwilling to put up with something, she was very clear about it. Her sanction for a prohibition was not that it would displease God or we would be punished or that somebody was watching us and taking all this down. No, it was, "I don't want you to do it, because I don't like it" or "Other people will be troubled." Respect for others, love for one another, and common decency were what she appealed to. I have no memory of ever being beaten as a punishment, and I cannot imagine it, although I realize now that was a rare situation in those days.

My mother had been brought up as an Episcopalian. Her grandmother had walked out of the Baptist Church in protest when she heard a preacher declare that he would rather see his daughter in her coffin than in a dance hall. Her act eventually gave the family a new start in the Episcopal Church, a break from traditional New England -dissent and Calvinism. My father's people were Universalists, and when we first moved to Sharon, he went to the Unitarian Church. Then he stayed away from the Unitarian Church and really had no respect for or interest in established religion. He was a Deist; he could not see that God cared whether he went to church on Sunday or not. God was up there, ruling that great universe, running the sun, the stars and the moon. It was a fascinating mystery, but the interior presence of God did not dawn on him as far as I know. In fact, he was angry, very angry, with those he regarded as people who did no real work of their own, with preachers who lived by stirring up other people and getting donations. He thought that was contemptible. Once he went to hear Billy Sunday just to see what he was like. The audience was told that when a big tin collecting plate went around, they were not to put in anything that made a noise. This made him very angry and put him off evangelists for life.

I was baptized as a baby in the Universalist Church. The only thing my parents told me about that is that I looked at the stained glass window and gurgled at it. One early memory of religion had to do with Girl Scouts, which I joined when I was ten. They had a rather general sense of one's duty to God and to country. Then when a coalition of Baptist and Congregational churches had a revival, I went with some of my friends. Night after night I was stirred, touched and a little frightened. People who believed in Jesus were asked to stand; I would remain seated. When the evangelist asked those who would like to join them also to stand, I would do that a little self-consciously. On the final night those who were just beginning to accept Jesus as Savior were to stand alone. I stood.

After that I went home and said I wanted to join the church. My mother said, "What church?" And I said, "Well, what about the Congregational Church?" I had friends who were Congregationalists. She did not like that very well and said, "No, none of your people are Congregationalists." So I gave up the idea for the time being.

The first time I ever attended a service in the Episcopal Church was at St. John's in Sharon on Easter Day, 1922 when I was fourteen. It was then a struggling mission, served by students from the Episcopal Theological School in Cambridge and by an occasional priest from the staff of St. Paul's Cathedral in Boston. My family were not churchgoers, but I had somehow become convinced that Easter was important and that I wanted to worship God on that day. I was not content with the children's service offered by one of the big churches in town. I wanted grownup worship concerned with something more than eggs and rabbits and potted plants, so I chose St. John's. I was a *tabula rasa*, an empty slate, with no idea what Eucharist was and very little of the story of the Cross and Resurrection.

I watched the goings-on, sometimes in trepidation, (did I belong here?), sometimes with outrage (people kneeling in public!) and in the end with awe and longing. Each small act and symbol, like the tiny pieces of a mosaic, went together to create a sign for me. The sanctuary with white things in it—hangings, lilies and linen—the sermon by a young priest from St. Paul's was about "Christly care"—how Jesus left the grave clothes neatly folded and not all in a mess. "He saw the linen cloths lying and the napkin which had been on his head not lying with the linen cloths but rolled up in a place by itself. He saw and believed."

The reverent, eager way the people approached the communion rail, expecting to receive something, and then their return in quiet contentment over a gift received. All of these spoke to me of a great glory and a purity, something holy up there, desirable, accessible and actually given. The sermon impressed me, not as an apologetic for the Resurrection, but as evidence that the young priest had thought about and drawn meaning from the smallest detail about Jesus. He cared so much about him that his smallest gesture was reverently and lovingly contemplated and drawn out for instruction.

"Maybe I should fold up my napkin better and not leave my room in such a mess. Maybe I should even be more faithful about my homework, and not have to do it on the train or streetcar on the way to school in Boston." I looked at all this as an outsider with awe and with longing, but except for one final incident or sign, I think I would have gone back to my home, like the disciples that Easter morning, impressed but still not believing that this glorious thing was real *for me*. This final sign was given me by a devout old lady with bad eyesight who greeted me as I left the church. She called me by my name and said, "Elizabeth, how nice to have you with us this morning. Won't you come back?" I have never forgotten her, nor have I ever willingly missed Sunday worship from that day to this.

Eventually I was instructed for Confirmation and, with my mother's help, braved the storm with my father. He claimed that I could not possibly know what I believed, that I was much too young to understand all that theology. My mother's reply was, "I've been confirmed and it didn't hurt me. I don't think it will hurt Elizabeth." In the end, he agreed. I borrowed some white shoes and a white veil from a friend. Bishop Babcock confirmed me and admitted me to Holy Communion.

Perhaps this is enough about beginnings, important as they are. At fifteen I was still adolescent and very much a product of my family and of my region. The next year brought me out a little from my background, into wider places.

Vocations

I remember with great pleasure the privilege of private drawing and painting lessons during my time at St. Mary's School in Peekskill, in a big old studio under the eaves. Mrs. Turney, who came in as a special teacher for the art class, had been a pupil of the painter Hugh Breckenridge from Philadelphia and was a member of the colorist school. She taught me how to see color everywhere. Shadows were not gray, for gray did not exist; they were pink and blue and green and every other kind of color. This prepared me for using a pure color palette later in art school with white in the middle, warm colors on one side, cool colors on the other, with never a sign of brown or black or ochre anywhere. For instance, if we wanted to paint fog, we put side by side tiny dots of white mixed with rose madder and tiny dots of white mixed with viridian. The effect was not flat but had depth and movement.

My teacher convinced me that I had some talent, but if I really wanted to be a painter I would have to start right off in art school, and I should not waste any time going to college. This fit in very well with my notions, but my family could not accept it. We came to a compromise and agreed that if I would go to college for a year, then they would send me to art school. So, after I graduated from St. Mary's, I entered Smith College in 1926 and had a rather irresponsible time amusing myself.

I studied what I wanted to, totally neglecting what I disliked—mathematics again. I had already had so much Latin grammar—Baker and Inglis and all the rest of it—at Girls Latin School that I decided not to go on with it, but I was weak-minded enough to take mathematics, a ridiculous decision, because I promptly began skipping all the classes. Furthermore, I had no intention of wearing out my brain—the binomial theorem again! But I also learned at Smith that Latin literature, like other literature, is real and alive, not just a collection of grammar rules. Although too late to register for Latin, I got hold of the text used in class—Cicero's *De Senectute* and *De Amicitia*—and read it on my own instead of doing my mathematics.

I remember also roaming over the beautiful countryside with my friends, playing a game called "Over, Under, Through or Across but Never Around." We would go out into the country, fix our eyes on a distant point and then make for it. Whatever was in the way had to make way for us! It was great fun. I did some riding, played some tennis and made some friends. Hearing President Alan Neilson in his beautiful Scottish voice read the lessons in the John M. Green Chapel, as well as the beautiful music, contributed to my enjoyment of worship. I had more opportunity to hear fine music there than ever before.

At the end of my freshman year, in keeping with my bargain with my family, I lived at home and had a very fruitful year's work in the Boston Museum School of the Fine Arts. That again opened a new world to me. We worked in charcoal from plaster casts all morning and in the afternoon had classes in design, theory of color, and perspective. We used the nearby Boston Art Museum for some of our work. I soon began to realize two things. One was that my shoulder, which had been knocked out of position by that accident several years before, was going to give me trouble in drawing. I could not work all morning in one position. The other was that, although good, I was not at the top of the class. So I began to think, "There are a lot of art schools around this country and a lot of people better than me, and I guess maybe I'm not going to be a great artist." Along with this awareness a new sense of vocation was beginning to show itself.

As I think about my growing sense of vocation in the religious life during that time, my mind goes back to my first impressions of women religious whom I met—first, to Sr. Martha of the Order of St. Anne with whom I once went shopping to buy those dreadful raspberry jam-filled doughnuts called "bismarcks," much enjoyed by Mother Louise. I caught a glimpse of Sr. Martha's face in repose, sunlit, framed by her starched white Second Order veil. She seemed to me to be transfigured, a beautiful image of peace and wholeness.

~

I was fascinated and repelled at the same time and in the back of my mind and heart there came a faint unacknowledged something linking me myself to this strange thing called "The Religious Life." (Early Days, 12)

~

Then there were the Sisters of St. Mary whom I met, of course, at St. Mary's School. I already had a bond of loyalty to the Order of St. Anne because I had become an Associate before I went away to school, and perhaps this kept me from fully appreciating the very different spirituality of the Sisters of St. Mary. At school the Sister Superior, who was also the principal, and our own corridor sisters took strict care of us. One I loved especially was Sr. Mary Vincent, "Little Sister" as she was called. She was gentle and understood us and our pranks enough not to resort constantly to punishments. Sr. Mary Antony, the Sister Superior, was impressive with her dark eyes and an almost coquettish manner along with a certain imperial quality. I can see her yet, bowing to each girl separately as we entered the refectory for dinner each night, each of us bowing in return. Her look was penetrating and her command of the school almost complete.

There were, however, ways of getting around the rules, even the honor rules. For instance, tightly fitted blouses were not allowed, but we used to pin our middies tightly around ourselves on one side only because we knew Sr. Mary Christine would stand on the other side of the line to inspect us as we filed into the refectory each day!

Our corridor sister, Sr. Dominica, took us very seriously and managed to put everything, including contraband and untidy rooms, into a theological perspective. I enjoyed debating it with her. I respected these women and had a sense of the depth of their vocation and their faithfulness, but I never felt drawn to join the Community of St. Mary. Nor did I commit myself to anything after graduating from St. Mary's School beyond a year of college before going to art school. Those years at Smith and the Boston Museum School of Fine Arts were, for me, experimental and marked by inner conflict about my future.

I am not sure quite how my monastic vocation revealed itself. I came to know the Sisters of St. Anne in Boston at Bowdoin Street through my discovery of the Church of St. John the Evangelist during my rambles around the city while still at the Girls' Latin School. My confessor was at that church and encouraged me. Little by little it became clearer and clearer that none of the other things I had tried were really what God was calling me to do. So I burst upon my family the astonishing news that entering the Order of St. Anne was what I wanted to do. It was one of the most terrible experiences of my whole life, because they were utterly shattered. My father felt that I was rejecting all that he had ever done for me, and one of my deep regrets is that I was never able to let him know how much I appreciated all that he did. My mother was heartbroken; like him she wanted to give me the best things in life and could see no sense at all in this crazy idea. I think she clung to the hope that I would not persevere with it.

In the end, in spite of everything, I packed a little bag one August day in 1928 and went to Boston to begin my novitiate at the Convent of St. Anne on Temple Street. My father was totally unable to accept it, disinherited me, and never saw me again, but my mother stayed with me. However much pain it gave her, she saw me through. Until my life profession she hoped and argued with me whenever she could to come home and come out, but after that she never tried again. She expected me to take my obligation as seriously as she herself had done in her marriage vows. And so I entered my life as a member of the Order of St. Anne.

~

Leaving home for the convent was the most painful, wretched time of my entire life—caught between family pressure—and pressure from the priest who directed me and was sure God was calling me to go at once, no matter what, and that any delay would be wrong, dangerous, almost apostasy. At 20, I was pretty naive. I have now a feeling that all the painful leavings [of my life] carry this burden as well as the burden of being steps towards the final leaving of death, so that I'm now coping with the remnant of that early transition plus the darkness, the shadow of the grave ahead. (To Tilden Edwards, July 22, 1979)

~

I was duly made a postulant, clothed as a novice and given the name Rachel. I would have kept my own baptismal name, but since there already was a Sr. Elizabeth in the order, I was required to change it. I rejected a little list of fancy names offered me by the Father Founder, Fr. Powell, SSJE. Marie Antoinette was one of them! Another was Paula Penelope. I took Rachel because it was from the

Old Testament, it was short and simple, and sounded down-to-earth.

There were about twelve or fifteen of us in the old house on Temple Street, located near the west end section of Boston where really poor people lived. For me there was a special lure in the idea of poverty. I began to take my share in the work of the convent, including learning to set type. At the back of the Temple Street house there was a printing press on which we published *Gems*, our little quarterly, along with a few other things.

I also learned to cook just a little, and every Saturday night I took part in our weekly expedition to the Boston Market. We carried baskets with us and stood silently at each barrow just before the market closed, hoping for handouts of what was left over. We always brought home enough for our needs and for the soup kitchens and the feeding programs of the Church of St. John the Evangelist. It was during the Depression years, and we tried to reach out to the poor and hungry in our neighborhood. I had never before seen poverty like that and had never experienced want.

I was quite happy doing all of that; at the same time I was able to carry on my interest in Latin. In 1930, two years after entering the convent, I was sent back to school, to Boston University, for my sophomore year of study in ancient languages. As I walked to school through the Common I saw men wrapped in newspapers who had slept on the benches all night. I was deeply moved by this and thought guiltily, "I've been called to poverty, but I have a nice clean, warm bed."

My last year at B.U. was an interesting one. One of the customs there was that members of the sororities ate their lunch together, while a big classroom was allotted for the use of those who were not members of those exclusive clubs. There I ate the lunch which I carried from the convent and met Blacks and Jews and one flaming Red Communist, Rema La Pousse. She and I used to spend the

entire lunch hour arguing, sometimes with our sand-
wiches left uneaten between us. I tried to convert her, and
she tried to convert me, but neither one of us won.

Another person I met there was Sarah Zesserson, a
devout Jew who began to teach me a little Hebrew. I sat
beside her in a Latin literature class. One time I practiced
writing out some sentences in Hebrew while the lecture
was going on—killing two birds with one stone, as usual!
When I began to write the word for God, she put out her
hand to stop me, saying, "We don't write that name." She
showed me the abbreviation the Jews use instead. She
also taught me a simple form of cursive Hebrew that I use
to this day.

While I was taking a course on Horace and Catullus,
one of the members of the Society of St. John the Evangelist, Fr. Johnson, a fine classical scholar, began reading
Horace with me. He would come creaking up the stairs in
his great heavy English boots to the convent library, and
there we read together. I loved it. Then one day one of the
sisters made a batch of cookies and brought us up a plate.
We had some; they were delicious. To my dismay, this incident marked the end of our doing Horace together. Fr.
Johnson's strict conscience rebuked him for self-indul-
gence, I suppose, and he wrote me a note saying he could
not continue our times together. I missed them.

From this perspective I see how the negative spirituality we were all taught, the Order of St. Anne and the
Society of St. John the Evangelist alike, cut us both out
from an innocent and life-giving joy in human companion-
ship and from the sharing of beauty, wit and humor—
things that would have been good for both of us. The
sisters had more sense about all this than the fathers.

I finished my college work and received my degree in
Ancient Languages in preparation for taking part in a new
foundation the Order of St. Anne had been invited to make
in Versailles, Kentucky, where we took over Margaret Hall

School, a boarding and day school. This started me on my real vocation, which is teaching.

While I am on this subject of vocation, I might mention that it has always been difficult for me to discern what place I should fill and how I should take part in movements for justice and for peace. I was always feeling guilty for not doing what somebody else was doing. I remember meeting Dorothy Day at a conference in the early 1930s. As we sat on the floor together while she prepared to be one of the next speakers, she said to me, "I've never spoken to an Episcopal audience before, what should I do?" I said, "Well, just don't talk about being a 'convert.' We think we're good Catholics, too!" She was very courteous about that and thanked me. When she got up to speak, however, I was abashed. I thought, "Who am I to give this woman any advice?"

As a speaker, Dorothy Day was tremendous, and she kept in touch with me after that. More and more I began to feel that she had found the right way to live the Gospel, and to think that perhaps I should leave the Order of St. Anne, where I was only junior professed, and join her. But I realized I would not be much of an asset. However, I talked with her about it, and she said, "No, you're in the right place. Stay where you are." I have cherished this advice all my life.

Margaret Hall School

When the Sisters of St. Anne went in the early 1930s to Versailles, Kentucky, to make a new foundation and reopen Margaret Hall School, it had amassed a mortgage of $23,000, which was a good deal of money in those days, and had been closed for a year. After we had struggled with it for a year or two, the Episcopal diocese of Lexington turned it over to us, mortgage and all.

~

I remember well my first sight of the school building. A narrow, cracked concrete walk led up to a wooden porch. The building itself was brick, rather like a factory, and covered with Virginia Creeper. An old stump served as a prop for a vigorous trumpet vine on one side of the front walk and beyond it some children were swinging....

Inside the house reeked of wet glue and whitewash. Mother Louise, who had arrived earlier in the summer, had determined to brighten the place up a bit and had had the dark brown wall paper covered with stable wash. Having no money, as well as no faculty, student body, nor experience in teaching or administering girls' schools (or any kind of schools) we were blissfully ignorant and could happily use our ingenuity to get things going. (Early Days. 12-13)

~

There were five of us, as I remember it, and not one was a qualified teacher. Mother Louise, who was in charge, was a well-educated Swedish woman who spoke several languages and had been admitted to the Bar. She was not a teacher nor much of an administrator, but she was a broad-minded, loving, cultivated person. In addition to Mother Louise and me, there were Sr. Winifred, a nurse from Newfoundland; Sr. Augusta, a bookkeeper; and Sr. Jeannette, who had had two years of art school without finishing high school. The first aspirant to join us was Tevis Camden, who became Sr. Ignatia. She was young, of great dignity, highly loved and respected in her home community of Versailles.

Together we undertook to run the school. The plan was for Mother Louise to direct the operation, leaving the academic work in charge of an academic head and a small staff of professional teachers. The religious were supposed to see to the children after school and on weekends, give them religious instruction, and be their friends. For me, it was a little disappointing at first to be stationed in a place like that. Most of the children were privileged, and I had felt so keenly about doing something for the poor. But it did not take me long, once there, to realize that I had a real vocation to the teaching into which I had been placed by direction of my superior. I learned to love it. I am grateful for my long career in teaching, and I think it has been what I was truly called to do, what I am gifted by God to do.

In 1934 Mother Louise was transferred to Kingston, Sr. Winifred left the order and Sr. Jeannette became superior. It was an eventful year for us. I had been given the job of principal. I was twenty-six years old, had no training as a school administrator or as any other kind of administrator. But we tackled it from scratch and made a good start, I think.

Under Mother Louise the original plan was for the sisters to take care of the children after school hours, to be responsible for the religious instruction and for Chapel, while the educational part would be carried out by a hired staff under a headmistress. Without any conscious recognition of making changes, as I took over as principal of the school in 1934, I began to envision a more holistic way of running the school in which all of us would take part in the work and the educational program would be integrated into the whole. I had my degree by then and did some teaching in history, English and Latin along with regular Christian doctrine classes.

Our own community had begun to grow during these early years. After Tevis Camden, other aspirants came; three of them stayed. Catherine Remley, the first of that group, came to us from South Carolina to teach in the Lower School. She had a degree from Teachers College and Union Theological Seminary in New York. After a year or two Catherine entered the Community and became Sr. Josephine. She continued to teach in the Lower School, eventually becoming its head. Sr. Marianne, who came directly into the novitiate without teaching for us first, was an experienced French teacher. Sr. Frances, a Latin teacher, served in that capacity in the school for a year or two before entering the novitiate. These three were crucial in creating the kind of school I had in mind where religious and faculty would work together in an educational endeavor aimed at competent work in preparation for college.

Elizabeth Freeland, the daughter of an army chaplain who had been educated mostly at home in her early years, came to us with a degree in Latin from Wellesley. Along with Latin she taught Christian doctrine and some history. As academic head, Elizabeth became one of my most important people in administering the school. Emily Hopkins joined us and became assistant principal. Both she and Elizabeth showed strong interest in and support for what we were trying to do as a school, and carried a great deal of the responsibility for thinking out, and then applying, our principles and goals.

During those early years after Elizabeth Freeland's arrival, we had an informal group of three or four of us, including Sr. Josephine, who used to meet regularly to work on the task of setting up a carefully planned, comprehensive scheme for Christian education for a girls' boarding school. We called our meetings "The Synod." I remember sitting out on the ground working together, with notes and papers blowing around. We tried to answer our own question: "What do we want the children to know and to be as Christians?"

Some specific points of discussion were: how to incorporate into the curriculum the knowledge and the experiences we believed important, such as liturgy and a strong knowledge of Bible stories, music and art; and how to help the girls develop a Christian understanding of themselves and of the world around them—including attitudes toward other races, responsibilities as citizens, and commitment to justice and peace. I felt that *every* academic department as well as every other facet of school life had a contribution to make to developing these attitudes and understandings. During this time we were becoming a distinctive kind of school: a church school striving to integrate liturgical practice, theology, history, literature, and spirituality with personal practice and social action.

The continuing interest of Frank Gavin, a professor of church history at General Theological Seminary, an Anglo-Catholic and an old friend, strengthened us as a faculty during the years before World War II. In the summer of 1934 he came to Versailles and gave a series of lectures at the Blue Grass Conference, sponsored by the diocese of Lexington. The morning lectures were on the Apostles Creed which he tackled backwards because he believed that it was easier to begin with "Amen" and work from there to the most difficult statement of all, "I believe in God." They were wonderful lectures; for me, they were life-giving. I had already begun a profound questioning of the old fashioned kind of Anglo-Catholicism I had been taught, and needed something more open to new ideas, more critical and responsive to psychological needs. He gave us just that.

Fr. Gavin's lectures formed the nucleus of our Christian doctrine curriculum and served as a basis for my course on the creed every year as long as I was at Margaret Hall. His evening lectures on the Old Testament prophets were equally important and nurturing for all of us. With his depth of learning, his breadth of vision and his warm, loving, humorous approach to all of us, he was a real guide and mentor. After the death in 1937 of Fr. Powell, our warden, we elected Fr. Frank on February 7, 1938, to take his place. Sadly, he was too ill at the time to respond to our letter and died on March 20, perhaps unaware of our choice. His death, a grief and blow to me, also left me without a spiritual director.

We elected his seminary classmate Fr. Whittemore, superior of the Order of the Holy Cross, as his successor. He agreed to take the position, he said, only because, first, he thought Frank would want him to and, secondly, he thought it would be temporary, until we could find somebody better. This was a miscalculation on his part for he remained until 1946, first as our warden, then as our first superior when we formed the Order of St. Helena in 1945.

During these first years of my work at the school, I was invited to become a member of the National Association of Principals of Schools for Girls, which also included deans of colleges for women. At the first meeting, they were discussing whether or not to give credit for courses in art, and, if so, what the requirements should be. One of the principals suggested that in the case of an established school it was one thing but that in those schools that were "new, small, and remote" more supervision should be exercised before such credits were given. I remember whispering to my companion, "I pray daily to become older, larger, and nearer!"

Their meetings gave me opportunity to meet some other heads of church schools for girls, notably Ophelia Carr of Stuart Hall, Staunton, Virginia. She took an interest in Margaret Hall School and offered to visit and give me some suggestions, as I was obviously still wet behind the ears as a principal. Miss Carr made her visit, stayed several days, looked at everything, talked with faculty and students, and made many wise suggestions, the first of which was—"Fix the place up, borrow some money. It needs to be brightened up."

So we borrowed enough money to paint and to spruce ourselves up in order to make it look a little more inviting. We had inherited from Sr. Ignatia's family some beautiful large furniture, suitable for the entrance hall and the reception rooms, and some fine rugs. By then the front part of the building looked quite attractive, and, with Miss Carr's encouragement, we were able eventually to do a little more in this line. As the school grew, I began to learn a little more about how to be a principal. A few days spent observing at Stuart Hall were of great benefit to me. I continued to look for guidance and advice from Ophelia Carr, who remained a friend of the school until the end of her tenure.

My active involvement in the National Association of Principals of Schools for Girls continued. Its yearly meetings brought me in touch with new ideas, procedures, theories of education and afforded the stimulation and value of talking with other heads of church schools. During these annual meetings of the NAPSG those of us representing Episcopal schools got together for breakfast and discussion. Out of this practice came the Episcopal School Association which subsequently had a day-long conference of its own just before that of the NAPSG.

Another significant factor in the developing life of the school was the role played by our refugee teachers. During those days before the outbreak of war in 1939 when Hitler's power was growing in Europe and posing its terrible threat to the Jews, we were in touch with a committee in New York that placed refugees—teachers, artists, and scientists. Every year we had at least one refugee teacher—some from Germany itself, others from Holland, Poland, Finland. Most of them were Jewish, and all of them were highly educated, cultivated people who contributed richly to the life of the school. I believed that if our children ate and prayed with Jews, they would not persecute them.

The first refugees to arrive were the Underwoods (a translation of their German name, Unterholtzner). Ludwig was a Doctor of Musicology from the University of Erlangen, Kathe a Jewish woman from Munich who spoke several languages. She shared the agony of her people, especially since only she, out of her whole birth family, had been able to get out of Germany. Her mother, who was with Kathe and Ludwig, was stopped at the border and never allowed out of Germany. That was a constant pain and grief for Mrs. Underwood who learned only at the end of the war that her mother had perished at Auschwitz. With their European point of view and standards of beauty, especially in music, the Underwoods made a tremendous contribution to the school.

Dr. Underwood arranged operas such as *The Bartered Bride, The Magic Flute,* and *Dido and Aeneas,* putting them in a range for children's voices. In order to stage them, he begged from local stores various materials such as castoff window shades to use in creating sets. He leapt from directing the chorus to the acting until he had a production which he could present with pride. Some years, instead of an opera, the girls presented a play, such as *Murder in the Cathedral* and *Everyman.* Every student was expected to take part in these yearly productions. They were not pap; all required hard work. And, of course, both the operettas and plays were presented with *éclat* to the local community each year.

Dr. Underwood made no demands for himself. He was always ready to help with any difficult physical work and had an ongoing concern about giving satisfaction to all of us at the school. Mrs. Underwood, fitted to teach languages, art, music and history, enjoyed working with the children in the Lower School. Although she came to all our Christian services and enjoyed praying with us, she could not leave her Jewish faith. I was glad for that. Dr. Underwood, a Roman Catholic, soon transferred his allegiance to the Episcopal Church. They stayed with us for a number of years.

Others followed, among them Simon Parmet, a Finnish composer, and his Polish wife. One of the refugee teachers, an Alsatian, had a very dramatic story. After her country was occupied by the Germans, she was arrested and taken to the nearest police station, where her passport was confiscated. When the official went into an inner room, leaving her passport on the desk, she seized it immediately, rushed out of the office to the nearest railway station and boarded the first train she saw. It happened to be going to Greece. There, somehow or other, she came into contact with the father of one of our students. Knowing that we were looking for a teacher of French and chemistry (a seemingly hopeless combination), he sent her to us. In this way one more refugee teacher contributed to the school's rich mix of peoples and cultures.

Just before the war began, in response to the anti-Semitism raising its head so dangerously in Germany and some echoes of it in our own country, our little school paper, called *"Pro Eis"* ("For Their Sakes," the motto of the Order of St. Anne), printed a cartoon by Sr. Jeannette showing a small child in the path of an approaching great wave with a swastika on it. About that same time we wrote an appeal to other church schools to help us bring at least one German-Jewish child out of Europe to our school. To further this, I went to a committee in New York that was helping refugees from Nazi Germany. (I was later told that the committee was Communist, but I do not know whether or not this was true). I remember looking through a few papers out of a whole stack showing persons needing refuge. Seeing those faces, reading their appeals, I said in despair, "Take them away; we can do only one!" We selected Luise Geng, and for the next two years we worked at clearing the way for her to come to us. During this time somebody said to me, "Do you know that you've been reported to the FBI?" When I answered no, she replied, "You'd be surprised if you knew who did it." I did not ask her because I did not want to know, but I am happy and proud and consider it a great honor to be listed as "a premature anti-Fascist."

Finally we succeeded in bringing Luise to the school, partly through efforts in London where she had a relative, partly through our own efforts, and partly through the intervention of Eleanor Roosevelt. Luise was greeted with great enthusiasm on her arrival at Margaret Hall. I remember saying beforehand to the girls in chapel, "Don't expect Luise to be perfect just because she is our 'refugee child.' She has the same right to be a stinker as you have!" She turned out to be loving, bright and great fun.

Luise had left behind her mother, who soon after was taken by the Nazis. When the Americans entered Auschwitz after the war was over, Luise's mother was released. She found her way back to her native city of Munich and eventually got in touch with us. We brought her to this country and gave her a job at Margaret Hall helping with the youngest children. One day she showed me a little packet of letters that she had received from me during all the time her daughter was a student at Margaret Hall. They were our reports on Luise. She said, "This is what saved my life." After Luise graduated from Margaret Hall, we sent her to college and to medical school. At Luise's graduation from medical school, her mother, a tiny German woman, sat beside me. She looked up at me and said, "I am thinking of the lowest day of my life and the highest. This is the highest." When I asked, "What was the lowest?", she answered, "The day the SS men came down those stairs."

As the situation in Europe became more and more menacing toward the United States, I began to realize that I had a big problem. Was I going to take part in and support a war? As I had been deeply influenced by Dorothy Day, I really believed only in some form of non-violent resistance. I talked this over and over again with some faculty, with staff members, and with my own community. One day Dr. Underwood took me in hand and spent about five hours arguing with me about non-violence, citing the time that Jesus threw the money changers out from the Temple. Based on his personal experience of life in Nazi Germany, Dr. Underwood was absolutely convinced that there was no way to stop Hitler except by force. He moved me from my rather weakly rooted pacifist position into one of unhappy acceptance of his position. I went through the war in that way, really believing that there was no alternative. I am not sure whether this was right or wrong, but it is what I did.

When the news came of the bombing of Pearl Harbor, it was Sunday and the girls were entertaining their boyfriends in the tea room, outside on the grounds and on the front porch. We rang the bell, calling them all together to the chapel (a redecorated games room in the basement between the swimming pool and the locker rooms). There I announced what had happened and asked them to kneel in prayer together. We sang a hymn and then went away in silent horror. It was a new experience of dread for me and for us all.

In the days that followed, the FBI began to investigate the Underwoods as possible enemy aliens. One day when they were away, the FBI men asked my permission to examine the Underwoods' living quarters. I tried to bar the way by saying, "They're here under our protection." A tall FBI man pulled out his credentials, showed them to me, and argued that if the Underwoods had not done anything wrong, they had nothing to fear. I responded, "Yes, but you can make mistakes." He challenged me to name one. "Well, I can't name one, but you're human so I know you make mistakes," was my answer. He melted a little at that and agreed, "Yes, it is perfectly true that we could make mistakes. But these are my orders, something that must be done."

I could not keep him from doing it, but I grieved about it and felt I had betrayed these friends. On their return, the Underwoods were both grieved and shocked, but nothing ever came of the search. Dr. Underwood was willing to enlist, to fight on the American side, but expressed the concern, "The only thing is, I don't want to kill my brother." His brother was still in Germany.

During these war years we continued to work hard to integrate the teachings of the church with Christian attitudes toward social needs and wrongs. Out of this focus came the yearly Conference Week, which proved to be one of our most significant ways of addressing these concerns. The first Conference Week, held before the war ended, dealt with the Ten Peace Points, which had been drawn up by the churches of Great Britain as a basis for a post-war world. The following one studied the Four Freedoms of Franklin Delano Roosevelt. The year before the school was racially integrated (1956), Conference Week focused on the race question with the purpose of helping the girls toward an understanding of why the Episcopal Church had said that no institution of the church could be segregated with regard to race. The whole energy and attention of the Upper School was directed to intensive study of whatever that year's topic might be, and over the years Conference Week proved to be an important way for helping us to bond as a community.

Over the years, along with enrichment of the curriculum, we gradually put together some ideas about discipline. We had begun without much idea of method or philosophy; the sisters simply tried to direct and discipline the girls the best way they knew how. As our system of discipline evolved, it included honor rules similar to those I had experienced in boarding school at St. Mary's, Peekskill. I felt it was not the job of a school to make rules against things that were wrong in themselves, such as cheating or stealing, because these were pastoral matters.

As part of the adoption of my proposal for a student council, with officers and some honor rules, each girl agreed to keep the honor rules or report herself. The Student Council, which alone could decide what to do about an infraction of an honor rule, met weekly to deal with reports and try to find ways of helping a student who was breaking the rules and failing to report herself. Usually they were able to solve a problem like that among themselves without ever telling me who it was. My argument was that if the girls took responsibility in this way for some of the disciplinary matters, the teachers would be free to do more interesting things with them.

Later on, through meeting Fr. Chalmers, OHC, from Kent School, we learned about that school's self-help program, developed by its headmaster, Fr. Sill, OHC. We adopted a form of this plan, and students became responsible for the housekeeping of the whole school, including the classrooms and living rooms and, of course, their own bedrooms. In addition, they helped with such mealtime jobs as table setting and clearing. Seniors supervised all of these work projects, just as they did at Kent. Juniors and sophomores also had assigned responsibilities for study halls and chapel lines. The plan seemed to catch on. At first there was opposition, especially among the parents, but the students on the whole enjoyed having that kind of work to do and the dignity of carrying responsibility. With many fewer supervisory tasks, the teachers were free to spend more time doing special things with the students—picnics, movies, plays and concerts.

At an interseminary conference at Nashotah House in 1947, I described our philosophy of discipline at Margaret Hall:

> Important as doctrinal instruction is, and especially for adolescents, a school is not a Christian school unless every subject is presented in the light of the Christian religion. History is the history of God's dealing with his people; the study of the English Bible and Prayer Book is literature belonging to the English classes as well as to the religion classes. Science is a study of God's handiwork. Languages are the expression of the instinct of communication which God has imparted in each soul so that it may share with other souls its vision of goodness. The study of language is vital to learning to understand other peoples....
>
> Current events must be taken into account constantly. It seems better to me not to use current events as if it were a subject like French, but to see to it that matters of national and international importance are prayed about in chapel and discussed in connection with the regular work in Christian doctrine, history, science....
>
> The principles by which a school is governed are also potent teaching agents. If stress is placed on the enormity of offenses because of the degree of inconvenience they cause adults rather than upon the real meaning of acts themselves, confusion about moral values or rebellion against restrictions will result. The role of participation by students in the manual work of the school and in the handling of disciplinary problems helps cultivate a sense of responsibility and of self-reliance in a very practical way.

We learned a lot from Fr. Sill at Kent: 'Give them a job and trust them. You'll see what will happen.' Human beings respond amazingly to being trusted. Perhaps that is because trust is at the heart of religion.

In the midst of all this activity and growth at Margaret Hall, while we were still living in the school without private quarters of our own, we started to sort out our aspira-

Margaret Hall School

tions as a religious community and out of this eventually
to begin a new religious order.

The Founding of the Order of St. Helena

I had become the Reverend Mother of the Convent of St. Anne in Kentucky upon the termination in 1938 of Sr. Jeannette's term of office. As I think back to the early years there, I realize they were an important stage in our development as a community, perhaps the first step of the real bonding that has to take place in monastic community in order to form our integrity as religious. Our struggles fused us together for mutual support and gave us a new sense of power, identity, and independence. There were three professed members—Ignatia and I, who were junior professed at the time, and Jeannette, who was life professed—and several novices. Although we were of very different temperaments, we shared a call to stand together and work out our relationship in God for the sake of the community, not for the sake of fulfilling our personal needs. This was one of our most important experiences of doing just that. Religious communities are not groups of women who merely fulfill one another's personal needs, but something far deeper than that.

Our order's Rule of Life forbade "particular friendships" (as they used to be called among the religious), and we spent a good deal of time discussing the meaning of this prohibition and trying to establish criteria for healthy and unhealthy relationships. Each of us wrote out our ideas on this distinction and then shared our papers. We had as yet very little knowledge of the psychological factors in homosexual relationships and tried to find our solutions instead through common sense, the demands of common life, and the dictates of moral theology as we understood it. For me, however, the study of moral theology was a trap and a swamp. The more I tried to figure out distinctions, the more confused I became. It was a long time before I had read enough contemporary psychology to get an objective view of this subject, which was such a touchy one in the 1930s—as it still is today.

So it was that when other religious joined us later, they entered a community that had gone through a good deal together, some more, some less, but the bonding at the heart of the community, those essential relationships of the original three, perhaps formed a pattern for the new order.

For some time a few of us, notably Sr. Ignatia and me, had experienced inner promptings toward a different form of monastic life. Both of us wanted much more monastic observance, more silence, and more time for retreats; we also wanted to recite the divine office in its totality. There were other issues troubling us as well. I took some of these matters to a meeting of the Super Chapter of the Order of St. Anne in 1945, a meeting of all the Reverend Mothers of the autonomous houses of the order. I was not satisfied with their response. When I returned from Denver and made my report to the sisters in Kentucky, I decided I needed to go and talk with Fr. Whittemore at Holy Cross to help me resolve what was becoming more and more of a problem. How could I continue in the Order of St. Anne, feeling as I did? I needed a different rule and a different spirit. The conclusion I reached was that I should consider leaving.

When I went to West Park to see Fr. Whittemore, we spent a morning discussing whether I should leave or stay. Fr. Whittemore would not allow me to talk about what else I would do until we had settled this basic question. In the end he advised me, "I think you should leave." We thrashed out the procedures by which I would do that. Then in the afternoon we tackled the question of my future. It was decided that I would discuss three possibilities with the sisters in Kentucky: they could remain in the Order of St. Anne and I would do something else; they could join with me and form a new active community in which the work of the school would be paramount; or we would start a new community living under the rule of the Order of the Holy Cross. This last option had been my wish from the very beginning of all this.

Rather quickly, within a week, everyone had agreed that we would leave *en masse*, and begin a new community under the direction of the Order of the Holy Cross and of Fr. Whittemore, its superior and our warden.

~

God did not give to any of us a founder's vision, a call to establish the pattern of a wholly new religious order in the Church. What He did give was much simpler but no less precious, because it was from Him a vocation to live as subjects in the monastic family founded by Father Huntington, under its Rule, and in obedience to its superior. For us to break this bond of obedience by becoming an independent order, would, I believe, be the end of what was begun when our order was founded. (Early Day, 21)

~

We would have a one-year probationary period in which each of us would be directly under Fr. Whittemore and follow the rule under his guidance.

~

Sr. Ignatia and I had designed a habit for our probation time....Since our wimples fell almost straight down from the tips of our chins, someone suggested that we looked

like goats; another said, "Lawrence of Arabia." Nobody
thought of the Little Flower, although once on a train
someone did ask me if I were a Carmelite. The dyed hab-
its were all slightly off-color, some blue, some purple,
some green, some brown. We were blissfully happy and
had our picture taken with the novice in her white veil in
the middle, looking like the Mother Superior, and Rusty,
the dog, at our feet. (Early Days, 21-22)

~

As we began to live under the new rule, it was pointed
out to us that we sisters would have to have separate
living quarters. We could not live scattered all over the
school without our own common chapel, refectory, common
room, and cells. At that time, fortunately, a house across
the street from the school went on the market. We bought
it, converted it into a convent with a little reception room,
a library, a chapel, a sacristy, and a big room, one end of
which was common room and the other a refectory. Upstairs were twelve little strangely-shaped cells, just about
large enough to get a bed and a desk into it. That was the
first convent of the Order of St. Helena.

Fr. Whittemore appointed me as Sister-in-Charge of the
house at Versailles. Later I was given the title of Prioress,
which I kept until my resignation in 1959, when I returned to the Mother House, by that time situated in Vails
Gate, New York (as it is today). Learning the new Rule required, among other things, that the daily office be sung
insofar as possible. Fr. Whittemore sent Br. Sidney Atkin-
son down to teach us how, and we had a wonderful time
with him; choir rehearsal was just a happy, brotherly/sis-
terly interchange as we began to learn the customs of the
Order of Holy Cross and the reasons behind them.

~

That first year under the O. H. C. Rule was a time of
deep quiet happiness, at least for me....We kept each
detail of the Rule with the greatest exactitude and made

many funny mistakes. For instance, we kept all the doors carefully closed, as our copy of the costumal directed, and did not learn for months that that provision had been changed. We made up every scrap of every missed devotion—visits to the Blessed Sacrament after meals, etc.

When it came to Good Friday I was a bit stumped as to how to get everything in. I did not know that the stations of the cross and the penitential psalms were not said on that day, nor that the three hours were counted for the required meditation and for spiritual reading. Consequently the time table I evolved was a marvelous sight. Fortunately I had a chance to submit it to the superior before trying to put the community through it. He explained kindly but with much amusement and cut about half the things off the list. (Early Days, 22)

~

We kept our rule very strictly and scrupulously. Fr. Whittemore used to tell us that we kept it far better than his own community did; in fact, we kept it too well for his purposes! He soon began to impose some flexibility upon us as we could not possibly do all that we were trying to do on one side of the street, and at the same time run the school and take our normal part in its life on the other. So we had to learn to sit more lightly to the rule and to use dispensations when common sense indicated.

During our year's probation, we could not tell anyone what rule we were keeping. This created opportunities for great guessing games among the students at the school, as we tried to make them think we might become female Jesuits! When, after a year's probation, the Chapter of Holy Cross allowed us to take their habit and rule, we made that decision public. We took off our transitional black habits and put on beautiful white mohair ones. However, we had to wait another year before being given the cross of the Order of the Holy Cross.

~

The novitiate began to grow and soon the new convent had all twelve of its cells occupied. Father Whittemore decided that we should have a new foundation, a Mother House in a quiet place separate from any active works. We made several expeditions in search of suitable property. Sr. Ignatia, Mrs. Hopkins, Betty Gatenbee and I went to look at some land in North Carolina, at Penland; we also looked at some beautiful old Shaker buildings in Kentucky not far from Versailles. But we finally decided to accept the offer of Bishop Gardiner of New Jersey to make use of some property in his diocese at Helmetta. Sr. Ignatia was appointed Sister-in-Charge of the new House.

We made many preparations for the new foundation, sharing with the Mother House vestments, beds, our refectory table, books from the library and chapel, pots and pans, etc. It was a day of joy and sorrow when the truck and the novices and sisters allocated to the new house drove out of the convent driveway. (Early Days, 25)

~

Fr. Whittemore continued to be our superior until the end of his term in 1954. After that in succession over the years came Bishop Campbell, Fr. Kroll, Fr. Turkington, Fr. Taylor, and Fr. Lynn. We did not become independent until 1975.

Recently, as I looked at a photograph of sisters and faculty taken some time in the late 1930s, I began to realize that the bonding in the community of which I wrote earlier was taking place at another level—the sisters with the staff and faculty. In our regular faculty meetings there was no difference between the sisters and the teachers; all had the same access, and the same opportunity for discussion and decision-making. At some point during this time, it came to my mind that I needed to have some way of obtaining faculty consent about terminating appointments. When the teachers met by themselves to discuss it, they said they did not want to have veto power but would like to choose a small committee of three whom I would agree to consult before terminating an appointment. I accepted that, and it seemed to work well.

Another very important element in the life of the school where we had our common ministry was our introduction as a group to Adlerian psychology and its application to our work. Dr. Rudolf Dreikurs came to work with us at the recommendation of the *Individual Psychology Bulletin* staff persons to whom I had turned for help when the adolescent girls in our boarding school were presenting us with some major problems. Faculty reaction to his impending presence, or of any other psychiatrist for that matter, was mixed. Some faculty members were skeptical and a bit fearful that he might be in total disagreement with our whole philosophy as a church school or that he might psychoanalyze us all. Some parents and children perceived it as a label of serious emotional disturbance being put on the girls. The difficulties with which we were dealing centered around some of the twelve and thirteen-year-olds who were very rebellious about school rules and rude to their teachers. They were failing in school work and trying to behave and dress like eighteen-year-olds. We had tried in every way we knew to appeal to their sense of reason as well as resorting to punishment, but their lack of positive response baffled us completely.

Dr. Dreikurs' first action was to talk with the students, then with all of us on the staff. He liked the open, frank atmosphere in the school. Pointing out to us that his visit was inevitably a somewhat disruptive influence, he also said that in no way did he want to create major upheaval in our system. We assured him that we were eager to hear his ideas and would tell him if they conflicted with our basic premise as a church school.

Dr. Dreikurs went on to describe the complete rebelliousness of the girls in question, their deep resentment of authority, their sense of being oppressed by both the older girls and faculty, and their feeling about lack of privileges. In other words, he said, they were reacting like a typical middle child. We knew that Dr. Dreikurs was right, that out of our fear of not being able to resolve the difficulties, we had become their adversaries. They, in turn, became even more resentful and rebellious because they felt trapped into living out that role. We had given them no way of proving themselves, of succeeding, of feeling good about themselves. They needed an advocate who would talk with them on a regular basis and show them ways of becoming contributing and congenial members of the group.

They also needed some special project through which they could receive positive recognition and feel a sense of accomplishment. Out of our fear and frustration, we had taken away all their extracurricular activities as discipline for failing grades in school work. That was the worst possible approach, for it exacerbated the situation. The girls' strong interest in dramatics provided a way of turning around the situation. They responded enthusiastically to an invitation to prepare and present a series of plays for the whole school and took on the project with few requests for help from teachers. They made up their own stories to dramatize and gave several different presentations during the year. After the shows, they served refreshments to the audience. As the year went on, their problems lessened and their school work improved.

Subsequently in our meetings with Dr. Dreikurs, we learned alternatives to the rewards and punishments approach to discipline, such as: win the child as a way to bring willingness to cooperate; encourage her; allow her to experience the logical consequences of disturbing the community. He helped us teachers to recognize the difference between punishment and logical consequences, to recognize punishment as imposed by someone else in response to an offense whereas logical consequences come directly out of the wrong action. For example, he pointed out that if a child came too late for supper, the logical consequence would be that she went without. With this approach, the person in authority can respond to the child with friendliness.

Of course, practicing this principle was not as easy as reaching an intellectual understanding of it. It is not easy to develop an attitude of consistent friendliness towards someone who has offended you and disregarded your needs, but it is certainly what the Christian gospel is calling us to do. The New Testament has many such teachings: "Render not evil for evil, nor railing for railing"; "Love your enemies"; while St. Paul says of charity that "it suffers long and is kind, and is not puffed up." Respect for others, patience, humility, compassion are all essential in developing healthy, strong relationships with children.

In working with the student council on the use of logical consequences, we devised ways in which girls who disrupted the common order could contribute some special work for the good of the whole community—gardening, housework, office work—that would also be related to their abilities. Sometimes a student council member talked with the individual in trouble to help her work towards an understanding of the rule broken. Every effort was made not to humiliate the person and to show compassion for her. This again was an expression of the teachings of the Christian gospel.

The "crushes" of some of the younger girls proved very difficult and demanding for the seniors who talked with Dr. Dreikurs about it. He explained to the staff that crushes, which are oppressive in nature, often reflect overindulgence of the "crusher" at home and an attempt by the child to establish a place for herself at the school. Dr. Dreikurs pointed out that being both kind and firm in dealing with crushes was—for most people—not an easy balance to achieve. Further, he warned us teachers to avoid becoming mother substitutes for a child because it immediately isolated the teacher from other teachers and brought her under the child's control.

In response to Dr. Dreikurs' sense of urgency about the need for class meetings, we made them a regular Friday afternoon feature. As he predicted, their value was soon evident. As a staff we explored the whole matter of perfectionism and its roots in the over-anxiety, worry, and pride which often take over when a religious seeks to live out her vows. We examined the nature of real humility, the direct facing up to our own strengths and weaknesses, and the admission of our need to rely on others as well as to be responsible to them. The last question we addressed with Dr. Dreikurs that year was the importance of academic success and failure at Margaret Hall. Although academic honors of different kinds were given for outstanding work, grades as such were not used. However, students were told their rank in their own class. At the same time, prizes and recognition for achievement in non-academic areas were given equal importance with academic honors.

In June of 1950 one of our staff members made possible a ten-day Child Guidance Conference for all our faculty members and a few guests under the direction of Eleanor Redwin, a psychologist and co-worker with Dr. Dreikurs at the Chicago Community Child Guidance Centers. Every morning we had a two-hour session, comprised of a talk by the psychologist on some concept of Adler's theory of child guidance and follow-up discussion. Afternoon sessions included a "case" presentation by each member of the conference and related discussion. In the evenings we spent another hour on some special topic: interpretation of painting, psychodrama, a sketch of the Child Guidance Centers, or dream interpretation.

It was a strenuous conference, but a most stimulating and profitable one that brought the group closer together in understanding. Through the talks and discussion, and also through the very techniques used in the conference, we gained a new insight into the need we all have for mutual acceptance and forbearance and for the kind of humility that makes a person able to face failures and mistakes without bitterness or discouragement. Surely all this is "not far from the Kingdom of God." And from it all the Margaret Hall faculty learned much that strengthened and helped us in our work with the children there.

Shift and Trauma

*I*n the mid-1950s I was trying to come to terms with another aspect of my vocation, namely, my sense of being drawn to a more contemplative form of life. Fr. Turkington, then our superior, suggested that I make my first trip to England. It was agreed that I would spend part of the time in communities working in education and part of it in some of the contemplative communities. I was also to take part in the annual Catholic Sociology Conference at Oxford.

I was quite apprehensive about my visits to the enclosed orders. Would I be sleeping on the floor and living on bread and water? However, all the contemplative communities that I visited received me warmly and fed me adequately, if not lavishly. At Fairacres and at Burnham Abbey alike I was given a cell within the enclosure, seated in the choir and included in all that went on. I shared in recreation on Sundays, walked about the garden, poked in the library, and talked a good deal with the Reverend Mother.

Fairacres is in Oxford, within sight of the spires but quite a distance out of the city. It has a good deal of land the sisters cultivate for their own use, and here and there in the grounds are small hermitages or pavilions where one can sit privately for conversation. I was deeply attracted to the life of silence and worship and to its solidarity, its deep sense of community at the most profound level. I was even attracted to joining it. It was a desire I never carried out, although it occurred to me a number of times during my life. It seemed to me, however, that because I was an American, not a European, my destiny lay on the other side of the ocean. I also felt that the part I had played in the founding of the Order of St. Helena meant that I should stay with it, no matter what.

At Burnham Abbey I met Mother Mary Columba of God, who seemed to me to be a kindred spirit. We had some great times talking together. She shared with me a good deal of the history of her community as we sat out in the garden in one of those summer houses on pivots I have never seen anywhere but in England. Here again I shared the whole life of the community and was not treated as an extern or a guest. Both experiences enlarged my horizons and deepened my sense of vocation to prayer.

In contrast to Fairacres, which had been founded early in the twentieth century by the Cowley Fathers and had always used an English daily office, the Sisters of the Precious Blood at Burnham Abbey sang theirs in Latin. The Eucharist was also in Latin. I enjoyed that because I could understand it and appreciate its beauty. All of the enclosed convents had lovely, beautifully tended gardens—with vegetable patches, fruit trees, bushes of all kinds—along with that lovely English grass. In spite of the fact that silence prevailed almost all of the time, I felt close to those communities and had many opportunities for talking at length and at leisure with the superiors. Since I was a visiting Sister-in-Charge, I was usually seated in the choir in the stalls next to the superior. I struggled to imitate whatever I saw her do—make the solemn bows, move when I was supposed to move, keep my hands under my scapular. I remember afterwards at Fairacres Mother Mary Clare asking me, "How did you know what to do?" I said, "Well, I looked at you! I copied you as well as I could."

I also made a visit to the Benedictine nuns at West Malling where I remember having it firmly fixed in my head that at some point I must seize the Abbess' hand and kiss her ring. Throughout our conversation there seemed to be no good opportunity to perform this rather mysterious ceremony, so at the very end I seized her hand, planted a kiss upon the ring, and fled!

Within a matter of months after my return to the United States and after a good deal of thought and prayer, I decided to resign as Principal of Margaret Hall and as Prioress of the convent, and return to the order's Mother House at Vails Gate, New York. This decision had been brewing for a real stretch of time. Not too long after the founding of the Order of St. Helena I had begun to realize how dependent the school was upon my leadership, and it worried me. By the time of my decision to resign, I had been at Margaret Hall for more than twenty-five years. I felt that unless I did so, it would be very difficult for my successor. I believed in the school; I wanted it to go on.

Even so, my exit from Margaret Hall School was very painful—saying goodbye to faculty, and children, and my sisters there. Finally, it was Fr. Hosea, the parish priest in Versailles, who came to the convent, brought me a rose and took me to the plane.

Once I arrived at Vails Gate, I was expected, by myself and everyone else, to take my place, quietly and happily. My place in the choir was changed. I had no special privileges; as a matter of fact, I had no special usefulness. No consideration was given in those days to the grieving that all of us go through when we leave a job or retire from something. I had been in Kentucky for twenty-eight years and had been principal of the school for twenty-five. It had been my whole life and now it was all gone. What a terrible time this was for me!

In those days, there was no provision for a sabbatical for a retiring superior as there is now. My experience in the years following 1959 was darkened by unacknowledged grief and by my isolation from the center of power and policy-making in my community. I suppose it was all part of a negative purgation, a necessary purgation, a weaning away from a dependence upon the power I had had, the scope of my activities and my self-centeredness. In short, it has taken and is taking a long time. At least now I think I see light at the end of the tunnel. I realize to some extent that the depth and stubbornness of my convictions and my tendency to absolutize my own sense of justice and mercy and not to listen sufficiently to the same things in others has made this work of weaning more painful and more discouraging. There is only the mercy, the warm love of God that carries any of us through this kind of darkness to the cleansing and simplifying and freeing that God wants it to produce in us.

I stumbled along, taking outside engagements one after another that year, waiting for a chance to begin life in the solitude of enclosure, which I did after that first year. I was still determined to find a way to a life of greater retirement and quietness. Fr. Whittemore encouraged me in this; it was his own hope for himself and in line with his own sense of vocation. I was greatly influenced by him and by the style with which he carried out at West Park his vocation to the enclosed life, but in the end I found it was not really suitable to our community. Sr. Ignatia and I lived for a while in the little house called St. Dominic's, with special hours for prayer and silence, three days of retreat each month, and restrictions about leaving the grounds. In the afternoons we were free to do as the others did, but we were still separated off in a way that was not good, I think, for the life of the community. Towards the end of this time I had an operation on my back, a laminectomy, at Massachusetts General Hospital in Boston, which relieved much of the pain I had been having. I returned to Vails Gate after some convalescent time in Sharon with my mother.

Soon after that, in 1962, I volunteered to go out to Holy Cross Mission in Bolahun, West Africa. The Holy Name Sisters were withdrawing, and the Holy Cross Fathers issued an emergency call for religious to go out to West Africa to help. Sr. Mary Michael went out first with Sr. Ignatia and one of the junior professed sisters. Sr. Frances and I were scheduled to relieve them after a few months, and we left the United States in September 1962.

Bolahun, West Africa

On our way to Bolahun Sr. Frances and I spent two weeks in England, visiting other communities there. We were based in Stepney, a small mission house of the Sisters of the Holy Name from Malvern Link. We were going out to replace members of that community who had staffed the work in Liberia for nearly thirty years and worked with the Order of the Holy Cross. Before we left England for Africa, I spent a week at Fairacres and had an opportunity to talk again with Mother Mary Clare about a contemplative vocation. Along with convincing me that I could go out as an active sister and still be faithful to a contemplative vocation, she helped me to see how I could do it. Her advice created an important link for me, keeping me from cutting my own development into compartments and allowing me to carry out to Africa all that I could of what I had lived and known in my two short years of enclosure at Vails Gate.

Part of my African experience was to find new forms of poverty, and I began to see poverty both as a good and as an evil. I began to see more clearly the *need* for holy poverty in world affairs, and I had a new vision of the depth and blessedness of holy poverty in the life of an individual.

Once in Bolahun I soon became aware that one of the fundamental issues in Africa in the early 1960s was adjustment to the modern world, a matter of necessity more than of choice. New forms of government, economics, and agriculture were alien to African tribal structure and created a growing instability in their society. The birthrate was high because children at an early age helped to carry the burden of work for the family to survive. As a consequence, relatively few of the Africans in Liberia were educated, making for limited leadership resources. The desperate need to train and educate potential leaders in government as well as in other fields was very apparent. I also learned that there were serious criticisms directed against the Christian missionaries in Africa, who were accused of disregarding African ways and African culture and of being paternalistic. Furthermore, the Africans experienced most westerners as very color-prejudiced. Yet there was also considerable recognition expressed by Africans of the constructive contribution of the missionaries, especially in education, medicine, and engineering.

Out of these impressions I came to believe that there were ways for white missionaries to serve and make a difference in some parts of Africa at that time. One of the significant reasons for mission work, I believed, was the widespread poverty. The missionaries from affluent countries should go to be poor *with* the poor in these places as well as to share their skills and riches. The missionary was called, I thought, to find Christ in Africa, to show love for him and to serve him there.

Bolahun, in the northwest corner of Liberia, had been affected by various influences outside of the country by the time I arrived in 1962. When the Holy Cross Fathers first went to Bolahun in 1922, they had to come on foot, since there were no roads connecting the town with the coast. (It was then an abandoned town under a Bandi clan chief.) The road, which was built in 1946, passed within seven miles of the school the Holy Cross Fathers had established, but despite these changes, great poverty still existed there.

It was at Bolahun that I first began to see in a new way that personal poverty is deprivation. Like most missionaries I approached the task with confidence, believing that as a Christian I had something to give and that the church had sent me to give it in this place of darkness and need.

My first glimpse of the desert from the plane window as I flew down the coast from Lisbon to Monrovia was shocking. Yellow-gray sand, bleached bone white under the beating sun, went down to the bitter blue sea without a break, with no vegetation to be seen anywhere. How had anyone survived crossing that desert? Then I realized that human beings had crossed it for centuries, for one reason or another—trade, sport, scientific knowledge, evangelization. Out of my inner sense of calling to follow in the footsteps of the earlier heroic missionaries, those of the nineteenth and early twentieth century, I felt exhilaration, excitement, and a certain dread. The words of Jesus in Matthew 28:19 ("All authority in heaven and on earth has been given to me. Go therefore and make disciples of all nations") echoed in my mind and heart.

My first impression when I arrived in Bolahun was that the mission was based on a paternalist model. Everything was under the direction of the white missionaries—the schools, the hospital, the leper colony, the outstations, the church—and they lived as much as possible in a western way. The Father Prior was the town chief. The liturgy was in English with interpreters—one Bandi, one Kisi—translating the words of the sermon. Although the hymns were in Bandi or Kisi, they were translations of English texts set to traditional western music. No native in the forty years of the mission's existence had entered the priesthood or the religious life, and no Africans had positions of top responsibility, despite the fact that some of the young men there had completed twelve years of school, gone on to Cuttington College, and went on to the United States for further study.

Early in my time at the mission I learned to go down to the girls' boarding compound and spend time in Mother Amy's little kitchen, talking with her. She was the matron in charge of the girls' compound and my African mother, whom I loved very much. One day Mother Amy was showing me how she could spin, using a little stone spindle on a palm fiber cord she twisted with her fingers against her thigh, and, lo and behold, a thread began to emerge. I tried to do it; of course I could not. And she said to me, "No, you can't do it because your mother didn't teach you how when you were little."

This was a piece of wisdom that stayed with me all through my time in Africa, and it helps me see now that the way the English sisters carried on their work in Bolahun had a great deal of wisdom to it. They had integrity; they made great sacrifices of health and strength. I respect their intelligence, their love and faithfulness, and their ingenuity in adaptation. But much more importantly, I think that few western people could have begun a ministry at that time by entering the Bandi way of life—customs about food, hygiene, housing, sexual conduct, courtesy, settlement of "palavers" (disputes), education, and so on. Those English sisters who were our predecessors looked after their own dietary and health needs in their own way, and trained a few Africans to help them do so. Without this help from the Africans, it is quite likely that few, if any, of them would have survived. Snakes, driver ants, scorpions, and the sawtooth edges of elephant grass, as well as an unfamiliar and upsetting diet, would probably have worn them down. Most likely they would have died of malaria, tuberculosis, or the terrible snail-borne scourge of bilharzia.

Placide Tempels, a Roman Catholic missionary, wrote a book in Flemish early in this century, then translated into French as *Philosophie Bantoue*. He shows that whereas the western world view is based on a central conviction that reason and intellect are the basis of culture and society, African tribal life is based upon a world view in which will and power are central. Even so, the Africans liked some of what they saw that British and Americans could do—reading, writing, curing diseases, running machines, building houses—and they were happy to have the village electrified so that the crossroads had a light from six to nine each evening and the study hall rooms of the school could be lighted. They also had a real desire to know more about the world that produced these things.

For me a crucial question was not how to become Africanized but how far, how soon, and by what means to offer windows on the West to the Africans—the Bandi, Kisi, and Loma people with whom we worked. I was concerned with how to keep both them and us from idealizing each others' ways and how to be open to growth and change without precipitating social chaos. I doubt that a painless and conflict-free way was possible, for the African world view was highly conservative and authoritarian. Its central sanctions came out of the will, including the will of both the ancestors and the extended family, clan, and tribe, and not alone out of the consensus of the living.

We sisters took over from the English nuns the work with girls and women. My initial eagerness, my fascination with the new sights, sounds, and smells, and my idealization of African culture quickly came up against my realization that the Africans were looking at me critically and finding me very lacking in the skills and abilities of real value in their culture. Physically I had certain important limitations; I could not carry things on my head, I could not see without glasses, I could not walk in the tropical heat without flagging. Furthermore, I did not know how to greet people properly according to their customs, how to give and receive gifts, how to buy rice. I could not even speak their language. In their eyes I was quite useless! I realized that I needed to learn from them the essential skills for survival and something of their value system if I was to help educate their children.

Soon after my arrival I was assigned, perhaps because it was the only useful thing I could do at that point, the job of watching beside the body of a baby who died a few hours after her birth and baptism. As I watched and prayed there, keeping the children and dogs away, I began to feel a little sense of doing *something* within the life of Africa and the life of the mission, a sense of the fullness of God's special presence there with some of his very poorest children. Eventually I did become more knowing about African ways, more mannerly according to their customs, but I never forgot those early months when all my taken-for-granted status vanished and left me naked: "Who is she, this white woman, and what can she do?"

Taking over proved to be a large order. We helped at the hospital and shared in "God palaver," that is, teaching religion to illiterate adults. The Sisters of the Holy Name had organized this "God palaver" for the two language groups, Bandi and Kisi. They had compiled a Bandi word list, collected a library, organized much of the evangelistic work in the surrounding area, going on treks into the bush with the Holy Cross Fathers. Sr. Hilary had put in years of skilled and devoted work in the hospital; Sr. Mary Prisca, who remained with us a few months to help us in the takeover, was in charge of the girls' boarding compound. Her knowledge of the inner workings of the mission was extensive. She knew everyone's name, of course, and also all of their families and their family history. She was also very conversant with African customs.

It is not surprising that when we first landed in Bolahun, the Africans expected us to be equally competent; we were compared to our predecessors and found wanting. The English sisters did it all so much better! It was painful and humiliating for us, and it took a long time to live through, but eventually we began to learn both how to do our own work along traditional ways and how to bring our own special experience and insight to the work. Since Sr. Mary Michael had already had two years of experience in Bolahun as a missionary, she was not as green as we were. When Sr. Frances and I arrived, she had already begun to make some changes. One dramatic change had to do with laundry. The sisters had been responsible for the priests' laundry for years. They brought their great bundles down from the monastery—sheets and habits and all the linen—to be washed by the women from the town and hung out on our back porch in the dry season and in the attic in the rainy season. The men tended to be late about all this, holding up the whole process and keeping us from going about our appointed business. One day Sr. Mary Michael laid down the law: "The next time you bring the laundry late, it isn't going to get done." The inevitable happened, and we transferred the laundry from our shoulders to theirs!

Sr. Mary Michael also began to modify the systems of control over the life of African Christians. No longer did a nun sit at the back of the church on Sunday to take roll call, and no longer was there a system of rewards—in the form of gifts of clothing—for those adult Christians whose church attendance and marital situations met the missionary standards. Another custom that tended to separate us from the townspeople was the requirement that anyone wishing to see the sisters was not allowed to approach the convent building, but had to stop at a small "palaver house" at the edge of the convent grounds and ring the bell. Someone would go out to speak with them there. Instead we began inviting the Africans who worked with us at the mission and could speak some English to come onto the front porch and to share afternoon tea with us there. Eventually, when Fr. Connor Lynn became prior, the mission adopted two further customs intended to change our relationship with the Africans to one of more equality and mutual respect. He "put a law" that no mission party should include one race only, and he also instituted a common breakfast party after Sunday Eucharist for all who wanted to come. The convent, the monastery and the missionary families took turns hosting this breakfast. Slowly the reforms were accepted, and eventually the contributions of the Americans began to receive some tentative approval.

I learned much from my co-workers at the mission, too. Nan McCleery, at the time a companion of our order who was teaching in the high school and living with us in the convent, played a crucial role in my life there. She was a brilliant teacher of history; a big woman with an immense capacity not only for intellectual work, but also for the domestic and technical. She was up on new ideas in practically every field that touched on our life and ministry. While we were still reading Hall and Maritain, she was reading Tillich, Camus, Sartre, and J. A. T. Robinson.

One day in the kitchen when she was making scones, she discovered my limitations in theological reading and study. She turned to me, her eyes flashing with indignation, and waved her wooden spoon at me to emphasize her words: "If you don't read anything but Hall and Maritain and Frederick Faber, you won't be able to talk with anyone except other Anglo-Catholics!" I have never forgotten that; it turned me around. I began to read Tillich and Camus, while in refectory J. A. T. Robinson's book, *Honest to God*, was read aloud to us.

Ever since, I have tried to be open to responsible theological writing, even when the point of view was very different from my own, and to move beyond my own rather rigid Thomism. The result is a somewhat open-ended theological stance. I do need to root my theology in scripture, but I need to read it as critically as I can to be aware of the tradition, and, as a monastic and a priest, to keep in mind the existence of an objective body of doctrine in the Anglican church. Liturgical texts I see as a special part of tradition. I understand my ordination to the priesthood as designating and authorizing me to be a public person in the church, a steward of its riches. In counseling, teaching, preaching, and spiritual direction I understand my calling to be a channel for the spiritual gifts God has given the church. It is not my job to invent new doctrines, however much I may be called and feel free to reinterpret tradition. All of this movement, which was problematic and obscure much of the time within me, began at the tip of Nan's wooden spoon.

I also learned in Africa a new kind of external poverty in my own surroundings, but much more so in the situation of the Africans. The effects of life-long malnutrition and parasitic disease were evident all around me. There were the victims of kwashiorkor, leprosy, yaws. I also saw the crowded, impoverished life of subsistence farmers, and I learned of their longing for food, medicine, and education for their children so that they would have more opportunities and more power.

Soon after my arrival I was made principal of the elementary school, which had an enrollment of 250 students, and given the direction of the in-service teacher training program for the elementary teachers. I also taught Christian doctrine in the high school. The teaching in the elementary schools was by rote, according to African custom. Throughout most of the school teaching was bilingual, but junior and senior high school students were taught only in English. Local teachers were used in the lower grades, but in the upper grades secular volunteers served as teachers. English was the official language of Liberia, and all schools were required to use it.

Dr. John Gay, a friend of the mission who was then beginning his experiments with the learning processes of Kpelle children in central Liberia, came from time to time to Bolahun to help us introduce the new math into our schools. He worked with the teachers and observed the classes. He also sponsored a vacation institute for teachers at Cuttington College where he was a professor of mathematics and philosophy. After extensive studies, he concluded that African schools needed a new approach to learning. He pointed out the generally inappropriate approach of the Americo-Liberian, as well as the American or European, educator to tribal people.

The government, dominated by educated Liberians from the coast, impinged upon tribal people at points where the African did not expect interference. For instance, tribal people would ask why a man should pay a tax because he lived in a house. Missionaries also tended to confuse the tribal men with their expectations (the law of monogamy being one example), and they sometimes showed insensitivity by not taking into account tribal ways of doing things. Most Liberian schools and the schools of our mission displayed similar defects, including the use of out-of-date American primers with references to hundreds of things outside the experience of the children, such as birthday parties, furnaces, and iceboxes. But the most serious problem of all was a verbal approach to learning.

African children learn by imitation. They are not told what to do, nor are they expected to question their elders or experiment with new ways. They are expected to watch and imitate. The aim of tribal education is to conserve the past, conform to community norms, and be a good provider. The child is taught first at home by being gradually introduced into the work of the family; then as a boy nears puberty, he is taken by the elders of the powerful Poro Society into the bush for initiation. (The Sande does the initiation with the girls.) Poro is powerful in West Africa, and because it operates secretly and with fearful sanctions, not many white people have been able to study it. Educated African men and women who are far enough away from tribal life to be able to discuss it objectively will sometimes tell a trusted westerner something about the bush school.

Its education is pragmatic, not theoretical, and intensifies what the child has already begun to learn at home and in the village, in order to prepare the child for responsible adult life. Boys are taught the history and lore of the tribe, and the right way to do things. After circumcision, which along with scarification was the main ceremony, they are taught songs and crafts along with other skills essential to survival in the bush—how to build a house, make a trap or fishnet, and how to clear and burn a field for rice. Boys are also prepared for their adult sexual role. This tribal teaching is by rote, and all divergence is punished.

All is taught in the traditional way, the way of their tribal ancestors, for preserving the tradition is more important than individual safety. This priority is evident in the practice of clitoridectomy, the counterpart of circumcision for the girls, which was often performed in unsanitary conditions and could result in tetanus infection and death. The operation can also result in lifelong difficulty with child-bearing and interfere with the ability to enjoy sexual intercourse. Yet a change in this custom has been stubbornly resisted, and the efforts of the missionaries to abolish the rite were deeply resented.

It is easy to see why American teachers had so much trouble dealing with their classes, especially when they tried to get the students to question or to come up with answers other than the one given in the text books or to give their own interpretation of things, which is all so natural to Americans. Problems arising in African life are solved by divination and witchcraft; dreams are a vehicle of instruction. Many Christian ministers in Africa find their calling through dreams. The ancestors teach through dreams. Conflicts are resolved by skilled arbiters who are familiar with the elaborate traditions of argumentation, the calling of witnesses, speeches and counterspeeches. The decision is made on the basis of which answers best accord with tribal tradition, not as a western judge would do, on the basis of the evidence. Both parties in the dispute usually do not deny their actions, but try to show that they were in accord with tradition. Folk tales in Africa often stress cleverness and wit and have for their hero a small, weak creature like a rabbit or spider who wins out over stronger opponents through tricks. The key to success in these tales, as in palavers or court cases, is the ability to out-talk and outwit others. Another thing these customs tell us is that society is regarded as basically competitive. Seldom do the characters in folk tales cooperate. It is the clever, lone person who wins in the end.

When children of the tribal people entered our mission school, they seemed to accomplish little at first except for a very limited command of English and some comprehension of how our school was run. I became aware that students often misused English, that they learned by rote and by guessing instead of by logic. Also, they appeared to have little use for the learning so attained. Dr. Gay, in his work with us, would point out the need of our African students for a way of coping with western culture that would allow them to retain their cultural heritage and exploit its hidden capacities for openness and growth. Their folk tales reveal not only a strong authoritarian strain, but also an inherent dislike for authority. The latter could be used to help the students develop a more critical approach to learning and eventually to government. Teachers needed to show the children that the scientific method is universal and knowledge is creative, leading to a fuller understanding of the world and helping people develop power to improve their own conditions. African languages are rich in potential; they are subtle and flexible. Through them the children could be led to form their own futures as well as maintain a continuity with the past. Dr. Gay very wisely perceived that it is dangerous for a society, for a people, for changes to be so quickly projected upon it that the young no longer have need nor use for the wisdom of the parents. The stability and bonding of the family are broken, while the young are emotionally traumatized and rootless.

One of the most abiding memories of my time in Bolahun has to do with the assassination of President John F. Kennedy. Shortly before I was due to go home on furlough, I was down in the girls' boarding compound one evening in their dining room where they had pushed back the tables and benches and were dancing to a victrola. A messenger came to me from the monastery to tell me that the President had been shot and killed, and the Governor of Texas had also been shot. I spun around to face the blackboard, then turned off the victrola, and slowly turned back to face the girls. I repeated the message I had been given, "My president has been killed. Will you come to the chapel with me and pray?"

We went silently into the chapel, an open structure with a thatched roof and parapet, and knelt down on the mats. The children crowded around me quietly, pressing their bodies against mine to give comfort and support. I felt so much at one with them, as I was aware of their grief for me. It was only later that I learned that they too felt grief over that assassination. As I was leaving the mission for furlough soon after, one of the young teachers said to me, "Sister, we think he died for us," and pointed out that for the first time in history, African flags were lowered as a sign of respect for a white man.

After we had prayed, I rose and started up the hill to the convent. I looked back in time to see the head girl throw back her head and start the wailing; it went on and on. The next day I suppose everybody, certainly everybody of importance in the village, came to say *"Bene ho,"* the Bandi words used for catastrophes great and small, for the stubbing of a toe, for the death of a mother. It means "Never mind," or "Cease to be upset," or "Be comforted," or "I am sorry."

Three days later when I went down to the girls' boarding compound again to do my usual job of calling the roll, the head girl interrupted me. She asked, "Sister, is your president dead?" I said, "Yes, Rosina, my president is dead." "Is he buried?" she asked. "Yes," I said, "he's buried." She asked me a third time, "Is he buried in the earth?" I said, "Yes, Rosina, he's buried in the earth." Then she said, "Then you must not grieve." This was her way of calling me back for the whole school community. It is customary among the Bandi people that when, for instance, a woman is bereaved, she may go back to her own people to grieve, but when the time of grieving is ended, somebody is sent from her village to call her to return. Grieving is controlled by custom. It is provided for, and it is also limited. I found it very helpful to be called back to my girls on the compound.

After two and a half very happy years in Bolahun, I was recalled by my community to return to the mother house at Vails Gate. It was a great blow. On my way out, my luggage in the truck, I said to the driver, "Don't take me past the school—I can't bear to see it again! Drive me through the hospital grounds." As we did that, I left Bolahun in tears. At my farewell banquet Chief Foday had mentioned something I had said to the teachers when I first arrived: "I've had a lot of experience in education, but I come from a different country, and I'm not sure how much help I can be to you. This is your country, these are your children, and I will not tell you what to do. We can talk about it." At the banquet, Chief Foday quoted this to me and added, "Now we know that she meant it." It was a wonderful send-off, a great help to recall it as I rode away from the school. They were sorry to see me go and, I think, resented it, but there was nothing anyone could do about it.

Travels in Europe

When I left Bolahun in 1965, it was customary for the Order of the Holy Cross to give a special trip to every missionary who had served some years and was returning home for good. For me the whole experience of visiting Great Britain and Europe and attending the Oxford Conference of Religious proved to be a valuable interlude as I moved back from tribal Africa to the United States. As I set out, what I had in my head and heart was the hope of returning to Africa after some study that would better fit me for understanding and responding to the new Africa I felt was emerging. I also desired to understand more how Vatican Council II and the new trends in theology, Bible, and liturgy were affecting Anglican religious communities. Attending the first Oxford Conference of Religious, meeting from June 28 to July 1, 1965, was to further my understanding of these various new trends and issues, since the topic was "The Religious Life and the World of Tomorrow." While there, I was to give a paper; I also hoped to meet friends.

The jeep that took me through the hospital grounds at Bolahun continued on to the border of Sierra Leone, not far from Bolahun, and on into that country where I spent a few days with the Roman Catholic Sisters of the Rosary. There I learned more than I ever wanted to know about the dangers of ritual murder, something they had coped with most recently in one of their schools and something I was to be faced with again on my return to Africa in 1969.

I went on from there to Freetown on the coast where I embarked for England at the same moment Gerald Durrell, the noted English naturalist and writer, was seeing his beautiful birds and beasts and reptiles safely lifted from the pier into the hold of our ship. We got glimpses of Durrell's creatures once in a while, but he was careful to exercise them only at mealtimes when no one else was on deck. I was interested to read later about his trip in Sierra Leone. On board I was assigned a cabin to myself and used my time to write the paper on "Obedience and Responsibility" I was to give at Oxford. At meals I was seated with some Roman Catholic sisters who were journeying to Great Britain from their mission. At Las Palmas the sailors and the nuns changed their tropical gear from white duck and light habits to European dark uniforms and habits. I knew at last that I had left tropical Africa behind.

On entering the harbor at Liverpool I had my first glimpse of changes in English style and custom—a group of long-haired young people in a small craft greeted us. They looked partly like boys and partly, because of their long hair, like girls. We saw more of this in Liverpool. Three years in Africa had not prepared me for the new styles!

I *was* prepared, however, to find in Europe and Great Britain interest in and hope for, as well as opposition to, the new currents of ideas in theology and spirituality, still vague in my own mind, about which I hoped to learn much more. I also expected to deal with some opposition to my ideas on obedience and responsibility.

Along with the questions in my mind about the level of awareness of new trends in the critical study of the Bible, in theology, and in liturgy, I also wondered how far these new ideas could take us in reevaluating and redefining. As I visited religious houses in England, both traditional ones and those beginning to experiment with new ways, I was both encouraged and challenged. I also gained a fresh appreciation of the work of some of the leading Anglo-Catholic scholars and religious, especially Donald Allchin, Mark Gibbard, SSJE, and Gilbert Shaw at Fairacres.

These visits to Anglican communities gave me a good opportunity to hear directly from them about the repercussions of Vatican II on their communities. I went first to Chester to stay a few days with the Community of the Holy Name. As the superior there had been in Bolahun, we had much in common. After Chester I went to Tymawr in Wales, then to Burnham Abbey near Windsor where I made a retreat, to Clewer to visit the Community of St. John the Baptist, to Wantage to the Community of the Sisters of St. Mary the Virgin, to Malvern Link to the Mother House of the Community of the Holy Name with whose sisters we had worked in Africa, to the Poor Clares in Oxfordshire, and then back to in Fairacres for a longer visit.

Regarding the effects on English religious life of the currents of change generated by Vatican II, the leadership of these communities was almost uniformly in favor of change and movement, especially liturgical change. Some were anchored in the long, beautiful, but cumbersome and outdated Sarum Rite for daily office and Eucharist. One at least was still using the Roman Catholic liturgy in Latin, and all were seeking greater simplicity and relevance in their liturgical life and looking to Rome for leadership in this. In several cases I discovered that their aspirations for reform were blocked by the authority of their warden or their chaplain general, who, as priests, had the oversight of their liturgy and the power to forbid changes. I am not sure how far this authority was embodied in the sisters' formularies or how far it was a matter of influence, but I was struck as I read over my notes (recorded day by day during that trip in a little red exercise book that has survived) by the existence of an "underclass" of religious, some of them formerly lay sisters in the English convents, who had so little control over the details of their own lives. For example, they were sometimes forbidden to read this or that new and supposedly potentially disturbing book, and confined to their rather limited and often rather battered and dreary convent libraries that had served generations of dedicated, hardworking, undereducated women.

In Oxford I had a chance to meet with Donald Allchin at Pusey House and to hear more from him about some of the concerns and ideas that were simmering in my head. His memorandum on the Anglican situation and the general situation in Christendom told me that he had done much thinking about these same matters. We talked a good deal about religious life in the United States. There was the question of enclosure—how valuable is it and how should it be practiced? He mentioned the possibility of enclosure alternating with time out of enclosure, as is the Eastern Orthodox practice. The "chapter of faults," he said, should be real or should be dropped. The question of obedience and authority is vital. The orders need a regular means of communication and perhaps a house of study somewhere, for, in his thinking, the study of Scripture and liturgy is basic to any renewal.

Before the Oxford Conference began, I went over to the Continent where, after buying a Volkswagen in Frankfort (the starting point of our trip), Sr. Mary Florence, OSH, and my niece Sandy Hosmer traveled with me through Germany, Switzerland, France, and Belgium. Our time there was focused on our interest in renewal in the Roman Catholic houses we visited and the special commitment to ecumenism of the religious communities at Imshausen, Darmstadt, Grandchamp, and Taizé, where we spent some time. The Protestant houses like Immhausen and Taizé, unlike the Roman Catholics and the Anglicans, had not inherited the negative spirituality of the medieval and post-Tridentine church. They had begun from scratch, most of them, not without knowledge of early tradition but with a freedom about it that the Roman Catholics could not, and most of the Anglicans did not, have. Ideas about being brides of Christ, "the world" as opposed to the cloister, reparation, merit, and celibacy as a bulwark against the sins of the flesh were absent from the formularies and the spirit of Immhausen and Taizé.

The Community of Immhausen in West Germany near the border of East Germany was founded by Vera von Trott, sister of Adam von Trott, a member of the German Resistance who had been executed by the Nazis. His simple monument, a tall slender wooden cross, dominates the grounds, and his story and the story of those who died in the same cause of resistance to Hitler are remembered there with devotion and love. The community was formed out of a group of young women whom Frau Vera taught during those terrible years after she fled from Berlin to the family farm for refuge after the execution of her brother Adam. After the war was over, they emerged from semi-hiding, and with a few men formed a joint community. The members of this small community prayed together in a beautiful underground chapel made out of the wine cellar of the old farmhouse. With their guests and fellow workers they ate their meals in the Great Hall.

At Darmstadt we visited the Protestant Sisters of St. Mary. They experience a different sort of community, highly centralized, matriarchal in the sense that the two superiors, Martyria and Basileia, seemed to do all the directing, educating, and forming of the new sisters. Its central motivation was reparation, with a specific focus on repentance for the sins against the Jews—an understandable and perhaps laudable motive for German women after World War II, but to me it seemed one-sided and negative. When I learned later about the approach of the Sisters of Grandchamp to this question, I liked it much better. They had sent a few French-speaking sisters to Germany to live a life of prayer and hospitality without any effort to teach or persuade, simply to share their worship, their friendship, and their small, poor house with

German people. When one of the latter complained, "Why have you come here? You hate us!" their reply was, "No, we don't hate you; we love you. That is why we are here."

Our next visit was to Herstelle, where we visited the monastery of the Holy Cross, a Benedictine community of women deeply interested in liturgy. We found a beautiful, simple but impressive chapel and liturgy, the latter still in Latin (Germanized by the priests—"sancti" became "zancti" and "quot quot" became "qvot qvot"). The sisters who met with us, Dame Sybilla Zenker and Dame Corona Bamberg, talked with us about the grille, which is required by canon law. Grasping the bars with her hands, one of them said, "This is wrong. It's wrong for us, and it's wrong for you. We've asked Rome to relieve us of the grille."

Their formation is based on scripture, liturgy, and the church fathers, a typically Benedictine spirituality and more positive, I think, than either the Jesuit or the scholastic approach. They were uncertain about the use of the vernacular in the Mass, but wanted to receive the Holy Communion in their hands. They understood little of Protestantism or Anglicanism, not knowing, for instance, that Anglicans claimed to have apostolic succession.

My first visit to Grandchamp in Switzerland near Neuchatel was brief, but prophetic, since the community was to play an important part in my life some years later. Grandchamp is a Protestant religious community, international in its composition and ecumenical in its vision. I was struck first by its setting—a valley broad and lovely on Lake Neuchatel, and buildings two hundred years old, once a farmhouse, a mill, and a dyer's cloth-drying place, made now into a chapel. An ecumenical retreat was going on while we were there, carefully prepared and introduced. The sisters were of such a fine spirit—generous, unassuming, intense, relaxed, profound, simple. Mother Marie, the *soeur responsable*, was not well; she seemed very frail. Lovely and intelligent, she seemed unified and holy. One sister said about her, "Our Mother *listens*, but she decides." All is discussed freely; this is based on the belief that God speaks to each person, and each person must speak aloud what God gives to her to say. They have an excellent library, both Protestant and Catholic writers, many classical sets as well as new books. The selection suggested respect for others and for ideas other than their own. Mother Marie, however, shrank from the revolutionary ideas of Bultmann!

The singing there was lovely, led by religious who obviously knew what they were doing. Soeur Yvonne spoke English very well; some others did also, but most did not. They often provided for three-day retreats over the weekend. The sisters do not usually conduct them but prepare for them and receive the guests. They do beautiful work in handcrafts, especially in weaving and icon painting. The meals are silent, and all the guests—male and female alike—share in refectory with the community, as at Darmstadt and Immhausen. The sisters wear a blue habit for work with a simple veil and sandals; for the Holy Communion they wear white habits and white veils, some of which are handwoven.

After leaving Grandchamp, we stayed over the weekend in Lyons with the Sisters of Notre Dame de Sion, then a night at a convent of Dominican sisters in du Thil before a brief visit at Taizé. The brothers exhorted us not to miss the church of St. Philibert in Tournus. It was indeed beautiful—Romanesque, made of warm rose stone inside with accents of dark brown, simple columns without capitals rising up to round arches. We went on from there to Autun and saw the equally beautiful Romansesque porch and chapter house of the cathedral.

From there our itinerary led to Cluny, Orléans, Chartres, and Paris. I took no part in the driving, but I did the navigating and the translating. Cluny was a sad place, but a most interesting one. Very little remains of the largest and most beautiful of the cathedrals in Europe.

After the Revolution it had been torn down, stone by stone, by peasants angry at the oppressive power of Cluny. The brothers at Taizé told us that when the monks first moved there, the surrounding farmers began to grumble, "First we had Cluny, and now *you!*" In response, the brothers created a collective, gathering together cattle and farm machinery and sharing its ownership, care, and use with the farmers of the area. The land and the buildings were to be held in common.

It was always difficult after we arrived at the edge of a town to find our way to the specific place we needed to go within the town, and Orléans was no exception. We arrived rather late and could not seem to figure out how to get from where we were to the small hotel where we were booked to spend the night. The three of us went to a little cafe and were immediately surrounded by a group of eager sailors, longing to help. We pored over the map together, and they finally made it clear to me what we should do. After I translated it into English for the drivers, we succeeded in finding our hotel. Next morning we started out fairly early, had breakfast at the hotel where we were delayed as we waited for our *café au lait*, croissant, and jam. The delay was caused by an American family who demanded toast and cornflakes. The waiters were rushing about in consternation in search of "des toasts," an unheard of commodity in a provincial French town.

From Orléans we went to Chartres. So much has been written about Chartres that one shrinks from competing with Huysmans and Henry Adams, but here are just a few brief recollections. The approach, the disparate towers rising up over the fields, my first step into the cathedral, hardly prepared me for the experience. As I hoisted my feet over the high sill into the darkness of Chartres, I could hardly take the next step. I felt as if two streams of power, luminous and alive, were rushing from those windows high up towards each other, lifting me up and holding me back at the same time. I could hardly breathe.

I spent most of my time that morning inside, looking at the windows. Later we went down to the crypt, saw the Dark Madonna, at the root of it all, and emerged at last to go outside and see the porches. I remember especially those elongated serene figures of queens and kings, tranquil and as if lighted from within. Then there was the figure of a woman just beginning her "lectio divina." She is opening her book, her gaze directed at it with concentration and confident expectation; she is still my image of contemplative prayer. We spent the whole day at the cathedral and then drove on to Paris, not even looking at Versailles as we went through. I could not bear putting the image of Versailles on top of my memories of Chartres.

In Paris we stayed with the Sisters of the Holy Family, Rue de Clichy. The morning after our arrival I went with Marguerite de Villebois to a meeting of *Forma Gregis*, a conference for novice mistresses. In spite of my weariness (my little red notebook says I was too "exhausted to take in much"), I have pages and pages of notes on the addresses and the discussions.

The first address was by Père Henri, OP, who, in addressing the issue of the formation of sisters for missionary work, described the new approach (since Vatican II) with its emphasis on the importance of entering another culture with respect, with a sense of the universality of the Christian message for the whole world. This new approach spoke out against attempting to change another culture into our own image, and instead called upon missionaries to teach salvation through Christ, not through particular devotions. From his perspective, conversion is an aspect of self-knowledge, knowledge of what God wills for a person. Père Henri urged his listeners to avoid self-reference and criticism of other people's point of view, and he spoke about a sense of the other, on a "level of grace."

Père Regamy followed with a talk on temperance and fasting, making the rather daunting statement that we must eat "morally," and then described several kinds of desire related to eating and drinking, only one of which was sinful. There was the physical reaction to hunger and fullness; there was the sense of being drawn to pleasant food; and there was sinful greed, which he said is a capital sin. This greed harms the spiritual life and leads us into sensuality, by which he meant too great a concern with feelings (as opposed to conscience and rationality) and desires for money. Fasting is a Christian duty and a practice that frees spiritual energy; it can also be used as an expression of love for our enemies, when we fast *for them.*

In the discussion that followed, the question of culture shock was raised. The French word for culture shock is *dépaysement,* being stripped of one's own sense of rootedness in a culture and a family. It is the opposite of "at-homeness" and especially affects new missionaries; I well remember my own. We need to prepare people to expect it and to be able to deal with it. From the discussion of the Vatican Council document, *De Ecclesia* ("On the Church"), emerged some cautious hope for an ecumenical attitude and approach to missions. Its theological emphasis on our oneness in Christ through baptism opened us to the idea that all Christians are one people; they have a diversity of gifts and functions, but are one in the history of salvation. Someone said, "We have left the impasse of no distinctions between Protestants and pagans behind"—an important approach in ecumenical relations.

It was also stressed that the evangelical councils of perfection, as they used to be called, are for everyone, not just for the religious. The call to holiness is normal for all Christians; it calls us to love, either married love or celibate love. Poverty, chastity, and obedience, ways in which all Christians participate in Christ, follow from our baptism. Religious, like all Christians, are bound to perfection—not for ourselves, but for the church and for the kingdom of God on earth.

After the conference was over, we left for Belgium where we stayed with the Community of Vita et Pax at

Schotenhof, a Roman Catholic order for women, Olivetans (White Benedictines). Because of their special interest in Orthodox music and liturgy, there is a beautiful and well-equipped small chapel for the Byzantine rite in their big chapel, the most beautiful of all the contemporary chapels we had seen. The sisters work in sculpture, tile mosaic, and embroidery, and their work is everywhere evident. While we were there, they sang a Slavonic liturgy, a very contemplative and beautiful hour-long service. The music was in eight parts; the celebrant was a priest from Maria Laach who served a parish of Ukrainian Uniats.

We went from there to Antwerp to turn in the Volkswagen, which was shipped home to the United States, and flew back to London on June 27, where we spent the night in a hotel near Paddington Station. Sandy left us to fly home the next day while Sr. Mary Florence and I went by train to attend the Oxford Conference of Religious.

Monastic Renewal

My weeks of travel in Europe and the time spent in various religious communities made me eager and ready for the Oxford Conference. When I arrived in Oxford, I had already heard many questions raised, new ideas launched, and had entered into new relationships and new experiences in liturgical prayer. I expected to find a quite different emphasis in the religious life at Oxford from that of the Roman Catholic communities we visited in Europe.

The Memorandum by Donald Allchin that had been sent out to all planning to attend the conference summed up very well what we were to find there:

> The Vatican Council has already made it clear that there is and has been a great ferment of thinking going on within the Roman Catholic Church which also has its effects on the religious life. One of the basic characteristics of this movement is a return to biblical ways of thinking about the Church and a rediscovery of the vitality and importance of the liturgy. In general this movement is encouraging a monastic renewal which is closely linked with it. Here also the tendency is to go back to the roots, to the essentials of things, and to set aside some of the proliferation of later centuries (multiplicity of devotions, orders, etc.).
>
> In monastic spirituality, for instance, it is the way in which the liturgy, Bible reading and mental prayer should feed and support one another which is being stressed rather than the differences between them. More generally there is a sort of ecumenical movement

amongst the Orders as they discover the underlying
unity of their calling....

One of the basic features of Christian thought in this
century and by no means only within the Roman
Catholic world has been the recovery of the eschatologi-
cal perspective; that is to say the Church lives, not only
looking backwards to its origins and the life and death
and resurrection of our Lord, but also looking forward to
the coming of God's kingdom at the end of all things.
The Church, therefore, becomes more and more aware of
itself as a pilgrim people on the move and sees its own
life as an anticipation of the coming kingdom. In the
Church the kingdom is already set up, and yet in the
Church the kingdom is not yet fully revealed. We live in
eager expectation.

In addition to Fr. Allchin, several other participants, in
my opinion, spoke prophetically. Mark Gibbard, SSJE,
shared with me his notes on "the fallow year" a time in
which his community would set aside many of its activities in order to spend more time together listening to one
another, praying together, and exploring the challenges
Vatican II had flung out to all Christians. I realized that
what I heard at the conference, with its concentration on
the specifics of monastic life and with Anglicans as its
leaders, would have some bearing on my community.

Hugh Bishop of the Community of the Resurrection, in
his opening address entitled "Religious Life: A Call to the
Love of God," focused on the conflict between modern and
traditional ideas about monastic life and called us to find
new ways to serve the world and the church. If we were to
accomplish that, we had to come to understand and accept
the world we lived in and appreciate its powers and to be
prepared to make radical changes in the form and spirit of
our community life, the affective source of our witness to
the world. In addressing the exaggerated claims often
made for the religious life, Fr. Bishop stated that the religious life is not the only school for Christian perfection,

for Christians in the world are often more heroic Christians than the religious.

He called on religious to concentrate on a simple, direct obedience to the gospels, like the apostles who left all straightway in order to live wholly for Jesus. Vows are not the essence of the religious life; the desert fathers had neither rule nor vow, and religious need to relate more to Gospel than to Law, less to obedience and more to love. The purpose of vows is to give us greater freedom to love. All three vows should be seen as ways of loving God and our brothers and sisters. The quality of love depends upon what inspires it. In contrast to the Jansenist influence in religious life, which tends to create a poverty that is grim and cold, and an obedience that is tyrannical and opposed to human dignity, Fr. Bishop described poverty and obedience as ways of loving God, ways of loving men and women in Christ, ways of learning to love things—to love God in his creation. Chastity is a human and natural quality, not something confined to the will or something "supernatural." It needs to be a real part of our experience as women and men.

The monastic rule, he said, should also be related to the customs of contemporary society, a society in which the role of women had entirely changed. Women religious should be allowed some of the same privileges as men—eating in public, attending concerts, plays, and movies, writing letters, and taking days off. He also encouraged reforming the habit and having a uniform suited to the work being done.

Benedict Heron, OSB, a Roman Catholic Olivetan monk, prior and novice master of his community, addressed the subject of adaptation in traditional orders. He pointed out the shortage of vocations in convents and monasteries of the Roman Catholic Church, and then asked us to look critically at our own understanding and practice of the three vows of poverty, chastity, and obedience. Calling for a more authentic poverty, he cited the

problem of large, luxurious monasteries in de-Christian-
ized France and the contrasting examples of new communities like the Little Brothers and Sisters of Jesus. In
speaking about chastity and celibacy, he emphasized the
need for young religious to develop affective maturity; for
them to achieve this would require greater freedom in relationships. He commended the reading of Aelred of
Rievaulx's treatise on spiritual friendship and recommended more frequent visits home, as well as the fostering of relationships between women and men religious for
the purpose of sharing in prayer and in one another's daily
life.

In Heron's view, obedience was the center of conflict in
the Roman Catholic Church at the time because its practices, along with their theoretical justification, came up
against much contemporary emphasis on individual freedom, democracy, and personal development. Indeed, false
ideas about obedience may result in infantilizing monks
and nuns and in stunting personalities. Fr. Heron stressed
the importance of communities learning how to share
authority and responsibility more widely, to find out in
dialogue God's will for an individual person. He invoked
the insight of Teilhard de Chardin in *The Divine Milieu*
that Christ calls each of us to share in the divine creativ-
ity, and that freedom goes with responsibility.

Most of all, it was heartening to hear what Benedict
Heron, along with many other of the men, had to say
about women. Like Hugh Bishop, he urged freedom for
women religious comparable to that of the men religious,
including more education for women religious whose intellectual development had been impeded and neglected. (I
had been very aware of this in my visits to some of the
English convents.) Grilles, he said, should come down in
convents; he found it illogical to restrict women but not
men in that way. He even tackled the question of the
wearing of habits by women religious and recommended
that there be no special clothing for those outside a con-

vent, except for a veil. (I myself have discarded the veil as a symbol of the subjection of women to men, as have most of my sisters.)

Next, Fr. Wilkins, SSM, began by saying, "Brothers, we are treading where we always trod." He attacked conservatism in the religious orders as "antique custom and medieval piety based on theory," a theory no longer tenable. Because, he said, "we shut ourselves up in medieval buildings and fancy dress, out of date and out of touch," we should not be surprised if the world ignored us. He echoed what I had heard from Père Henri and others in Paris about the religious need for work in missions. "We don't go to teach the heathen. We go to listen and to learn." Suffering, he said, is not just putting up with pain, but allowing things to be done to you. Action and passion are two aspects of one thing. We are to wait for God to show us new ways of service; meanwhile, he said, "let us cultivate our gardens." He identified the loss of members in many communities as a symptom of the retreat of Christendom, and cited the English Prayer Book's continuing practice of praying for the Queen and not for the Prime Minister as one more sign of how out of touch Anglicans were with the political realities of the day.

Fr. Peter, OSB, an Anglican Benedictine, accused us of the heresy of dualism in having "laid the flesh so strongly against the spirit." He envisioned more small and informal communities without many rules and without the separation of those in authority from the rank and file, where people can live together in ordinary joys and troubles and go out to work in schools, in playgrounds, in prisons— wherever young people are.

Br. Gerard of Taizé gave us an overview of his interdenominational and international community with its vocation to search for the visible unity of Christians. Each member is fully involved in this vocation. In their understanding of the threefold vow, Br. Gerard said they avoided the words "poverty, chastity, and obedience" because all persons are called to these. Instead they speak of celibacy, the acceptance of the prior's authority, and community of goods; this last vow includes all goods, including artistic goods. Since Taizé has no endowment and solicits no gifts, the brethren live by their work, normally manual labor. Their rule, written after the community's foundation, has been adopted by the Sisters of Grandchamp. Taizé does not see its community as permanent; God may some day melt it into a more universal situation. The spirituality of Taizé is centered on the Transfiguration. "We and our neighbors and institutions are in darkness. We fix our eyes on the Light of Christ, the Morning Star who rises to eliminate and transfigure all things."

Fr. Michael Fisher, SSF, an Anglican Franciscan, pointed out that although the large majority of religious are women, all the main speakers at the conference were men. He deplored the frequent failure of communities to use the gifts of creative and well-educated women. Many of the practices of sisters he described as both burdensome and relatively meaningless, their cumbersome habits a clear example of this. While praising the work of women religious, especially their work with the poor and disadvantaged, he suggested that they reach out to others, such as professionals and office workers whose spiritual needs are often as great as the needs of the poor, for these men and women are in "the rat race." Our ministry should not be confined to church groups; we should be able to offer service to the "church latent." To do this, he pointed out, we needed to be realistic, to be in touch with contemporary thinking in order to be able to express the church manifest, the kingdom of God on earth.

My own paper focused on the effect of our formation in obedience on the individual members of our religious communities and on our corporate witness to the world in such areas as ecumenism, race relations, and Christian citizenship. I discussed the impact of two distinct views of obedience: the Augustinian, which presents obedience as a free and loving acceptance of the Word of God and, in opposition to that, the juridical positivism of the nineteenth century that is based on the false notion that God does not command something because it is right, but rather it is right because God commands it. This second view of obedience often produces domineering superiors and a tendency in subjects to avoid responsibility and develop neurotic and rebellious behavior. Its substitution of exterior surrender for interior consent inhibits the formation of a genuine common witness by a community.

In presenting the issue of obedience and personal judgment, I challenged the use of such misleading terms as "blind obedience" and "submission of judgment." I wrote: "To speak of 'blind obedience' is to speak of an imperfection, not an ideal. It is only because of the darkness sin causes in our minds that Christian obedience is ever blind. All men have sometimes to obey without knowing the reason why because of their limitations or their weaknesses. Perfect obedience, on the other hand, expands our hearts and enlightens our minds." I pointed out that the expression "submission of judgment" is equally troublesome and misleading, and has led to a kind of caricature of religious life in popular novels. A religious is not bound to agree with a superior or to believe the rule infallible, for that would render inoperative the safeguards of conscience. An order that may seem unwise, but does not lead a person into sin, must be obeyed. Acknowledging the possibility of error in personal judgment can help the religious to perfect obedience while at the same time maintaining personal convictions about right.

The giving of self through the vows means sacrifice and loss and acceptance of the fact that many latent capabilities must go unrealized. However, the positive aspect is that self is to be valued and the freedom coming out of obedience—which is more than *not doing* certain things— enables individuals to develop mind and will to their fullest potential. Religious orders should foster personal

integration and development by living under the new commandment of love, for a false view of obedience harms the
individual religious. For that reason, religious community
rules should allow members to express conscience, to discuss their concerns with other members, to seek spiritual
guidance outside the community when the need is felt,
and to recommend ways of change and reform.

In the concluding section on obedience and our corporate witness, I pointed out that our ability to address
the needs of the world without is dependent upon our
openness of mind to new, even disturbing, ideas and on
our freedom in discussing them. In order to work effectively in the larger community, religious must express an
open-minded, informed approach to other people and cultures, working in partnership with them. This is possible
only if a religious community has reached a common mind
that frees the community to speak to others out of Christ-
like love.

In a later discussion group I led on my paper, dissent
was considerably outweighed by agreement with my
views. Several of the communities invited me to visit them
and present my paper to their membership. I was able to
accept several of these invitations on my way south to
take ship for home on the Holland-American Line. As I
look back now over what I have written on the Oxford
Conference and reflect on its long-term effect, I come up
with a confused picture. Examining the religious life in
general, especially in the present day, I see some obvious
results of renewal. In the Roman Catholic Church, sisters
have been required to reform their habits; no more do we
see those great sails of headdresses, no more starched
linen covering heads and foreheads completely, no more
yards of billowing woolen skirts. They have not entirely
discarded their habits in exchange for a ring and a cross,
but modern habits and veils are much less cumbersome
and conspicuous. The same is true for some Anglicans, although the modification of habit is much less widespread

among us than among the Roman Catholics. A very few of us have entirely abandoned the required wearing of the habit. My own community and the Sisters of St. Mary in Sewanee have perhaps the most latitude.

The religious habit was one of the earliest questions raised at Oxford and one that brought debate and disagreement. What we look like is important, especially to women, but it is not basic. I know how naked I felt in 1967 when I first took off my habit and veil and went to see a Fellini movie in Toronto where I was studying! On the other hand, I was enormously relieved to be able to go into a movie house and take my seat without being looked at. Being totally inconspicuous was a wonderful feeling. It is very important to remember that, for a religious, clothing is far less basic than what our vows, our prayer, our liturgy, and our work say about our love for the world.

One of the most striking results of renewal for Roman Catholics has been their growing sense of freedom of conscience. More and more frequently one hears about members of their religious communities challenging publicly some Vatican directive or policy. This would not have been possible in 1965, I feel sure. It has come about, not so much through changing the religious habit, as through changing the education, ministry, and work of sisters. As they have entered more deeply into the world around them and prepared themselves for professional work, they have developed a growing impulse to express themselves freely about many different matters, including dress.

It is not strange that most of the initiative for change at Oxford came from men, but as I visited convents and talked with individual superiors and the rank and file members, I perceived the timidity and uncertainty of so many women religious. There were exceptions: Mother Annys of Clewer and Mother Mary Clare of Fairacres especially stand out, and some of the Sisters of Wantage exercised vigorous leadership.

Fr. Gilbert Shaw at Fairacres pointed out to me that my own community needed to rethink its relationship with the Order of the Holy Cross. Was it right, he asked, that we should be without our own elected superior? He thought the women were not given sufficient scope. As he talked with me, he gave much emphasis to power and emotion and pointed out that the "dark night of the soul" is a necessary experience for arriving at unity and reconciliation. Reconciliation is a gift; we cannot do it ourselves. We cannot fill up what is wanting; Christ does that. This kind of theology, I think, lay at the root of the decision of the Fairacres sisters to exclude from their rule the term "reparation," with its suggestion that we can fill up something lacking in the suffering of Jesus on the Cross and that our fasts and penances have power to do this for others.

In comparison with the Oxford Conference of 1965, from which I came away strengthened in my vocation, most of us who attended the second one in 1967 felt that it offered less stimulation, a less intense feeling of joy and spontaneity in the corporate worship, and a more relaxed attitude on the part of the religious in attendance. The first conference had taken place in a time of high tension. New and threatening and interesting ideas, challenges and even accusations were hurled at us; totally new forms of eucharistic worship were sprung upon us. We had no time then to think out or evaluate our reactions. Some people were stimulated, relieved, and thrilled, as I was, at all the wonderful new vistas opening before us and glad that at last pent-up doubts or questionings could be brought out and looked at.

A great deal of quiet and purposeful thinking had obviously taken place in the intervening two years, so that the second conference seemed more of a "reporting back" on things accomplished than an effort to get things unstuck. New experiments in liturgy, in the use of sacramental confession, chapter of faults, new kinds of work in cooperation with other communities, and a few not very drastic revisions of habits were brought to that conference as topics of discussions or reports of things accomplished.

The schedule in 1967 was overcrowded, and for many the worship fell flat. St. Mary's university church was built for a medieval mass celebrated at a high altar far beyond a screened-off choir, but was not well adapted to contemporary liturgy. By permission of the Bishop of Oxford we used the proposed new rite for the Church of England. It was certainly an advance over 1662 but lacked the beauty, simplicity, and directness of movement, I thought, of the Fairacres and West Malling rites and the richness of the rite of South India. Similarly, the presentations lacked the compelling qualities both in subject matter and delivery of the earlier meeting. At the end I felt disappointment that it had not been more ecumenical and made a greater effort to include Protestant religious and deaconesses. I also thought that any later conference should be held in a place where the Eucharist and the daily offices were done in a contemporary form.

All these years later I still have uncertainties about the real accomplishments of the two Oxford Conferencess. The words of Mother Mary Clare, SLG, of Fairacres come to mind in response to my concerns and disappointments about the apparent slowness of change and growth in the religious life:

> We must try to understand the meaning of the age in which we are called to bear witness. We must accept the fact that this is an age in which the cloth is being unwoven. It is therefore no good trying to patch. We must, rather, set up the loom on which coming generations may weave new cloth according to the pattern God provides.

For me, her words still speak in a prophetic voice.

At this point I interrupted the dictating of this book to take one of my daily walks around a block or two, part of my therapy. My head was full of what I had been working with—the ideas, initiatives, criticisms, challenges projected at that first Oxford Conference on Religious. As I pondered what I had been reading and dictating, I tried to answer the first of the challenges: that we should know, understand, and love the world around us. My first question to myself was, "How have I entered into the world around me today? How deeply do I understand that world? How do I see it as God's beloved creation and the place of our witness and ministry as Christians? Have I changed since 1965?"

It is a different world in many ways from the world that I saw around me at the Oxford Conferences. Then I saw the world from the perspective of Europe and Africa rather than of the United States, which I had not seen, except for a brief furlough, for three years. At the Paris meeting especially, I was reassured about the importance of including Africa and the Third World areas in all our thinking and praying and eventually in our action, and I was stimulated by the new theological emphases on the goodness and preciousness of the world and its peoples. Today as I walk around, I am aware of the sights and sounds and smells of this great city of New York and of our area near the welfare hotels on 28th Street: streets filled with homeless people, some asleep in doorways with their whisky bottles half-concealed in paper bags beside them; some of them panhandling, not always courteously or patiently; some of them teenage mothers pulling small children in shopping carts filled with laundry. The small repair shops and cheap restaurants are beginning to yield to boutiques and little holes in the wall selling greeting cards and party paraphernalia, decorations and flimsies of bright colors but of no discernible usefulness. Folks hurry by me going to their jobs at Bellevue Hospital a few blocks away and to various midtown offices and work places.

Do I see all this as God's beloved creation? How can I love and honor it? What have I learned since 1965 about the world around me? I cannot answer this here but will try to answer it as I go along—here I will simply report that I see it much more clearly in its fragility. How can it last? I ask with Julian, "Do I hear God reply: 'It lasts because I made it, I keep it and I love it?'" In my prayer time I can try to hear what God is asking me to do about it. I can also reflect upon the responses of my sister religious who are asking the same questions and striving to respond in prayer and in ministry, in seminary, in the South Bronx, and in hospices for the dying where they work.

Transition and Change

Upon my return from Africa in 1965 after attending the first Oxford Conference, I was made novice mistress at our mother house at Vails Gate, an office I held only for a year. After that I spent a lot of time at loose ends with little to do. I found myself a Sunday school class to teach at St. George's in Newburgh and an inquirers' class at St. John's in Cornwall; but for the most part, especially after I was taken out as novice mistress, I was lonely and unhappy. My own solution to this situation was to go back to school to do some of the study that I had determined to do while I was still in Bolahun—catching up with the new ideas in theology and Bible study. I also saw it as a way to get retooled for a possible return to Africa. I wanted to undertake this study either in a Roman Catholic or Protestant institution rather than an Episcopal seminary.

My first year of study was in Toronto where I lived with the Sisters of the Church, helping with the care of the older girls and teaching some Latin and some Christian doctrine. At Trinity College I took two courses, one in New Testament with John Hurd and one in Anglican theology with Eugene Fairweather. At Emmanuel, the college of the United Church of Christ in Canada, I studied both ethics and Old Testament ethics, and at St. Michael's, a Roman Catholic college, I took a course in church and society. Working away at theology was great. John Ryan, then a member of the Order of Holy Cross, was in residence there too. Some good advice from him about courses and professors helped me to end up with a very satisfying program. I appreciated and enjoyed both my professors and my fellow students. In many ways it was a good year.

Going back to school as a graduate student after many years as a high school teacher and administrator in the United States and in West Africa had showed me the challenges the religious life must face in the world today. These challenges to the spiritual and theological bases of the religious life come not only from the world of technology, sociology, and psychology, but also from those very worlds that used to feed and support us—from theology and Scripture study itself. I knew that the life of total dedication to God by vows, renouncing "the world" and taking up formal obligations to poverty, chastity, and obedience, is an ancient way of life in the church. Its spirituality is not meant to be an end in itself, but it can become so and interfere with the atmosphere of prayer and contemplation that must be cultivated within the community for its members. Religious are called to be disciplined people who can serve the needs of the world in a special way because of their freedom from marriage vows, possessions, personal status, and power.

Without defaulting on our obligation to God, to each other in community, and to those we work with and those we serve, we were struggling for a new rationale for the religious life. Painful conflicts arose between the need for personal maturity and a sense of responsibility for others who may be changing at a different rate or in a different direction from ourselves. In many communities life-professed members began leaving after many years in monastic life, while ours tried to become more aware of changes and more prepared for new ministries by sending some of us to school. We were also seeking a consensus on our formularies, our work, and our form of government. It has been a long journey and one we have not yet completed. Indeed, I am sure we never will, though I hope we have begun to find a middle way between clinging to the old negative spirituality and getting lost in the fog of "anything goes if it feels good to you."

After my year of study in Canada, I took up residence at Union Theological Seminary in New York to complete a master's degree in the literature and religion of the Bible, with a minor in African studies at Columbia. Theology during those two years was a side issue for me. I wrote my thesis on "Biblical Attitudes to Poverty," struggling with the idea of poverty as a good. I had to struggle, in fact, not only with myself, but also with my adviser and the faculty at Union, none of whom believed that poverty could ever be "a good." One of my efforts to deal with this issue stimulated my friend Dr. Barry Wood to arrange an invitation for me to write for *Psychoanalytic Review*, in their column called "Other Voices," a short paper entitled "Poverty and Human Growth."

My working premise was that both economic privation and spiritual poverty are the antithesis of human growth and life. I pointed out that, paradoxically, poverty has been related traditionally to blessedness as in the first beatitude of the Sermon on the Mount (Matthew 5:3). To be "poor in spirit" does not signify any kind of weakness, but rather an inner attitude of humility, moderation, and concern about others. The reality that this poverty of spirit sometimes appears in the midst of deep material privation in the form of an enriching simplicity of life raises the question, Can severe external poverty be life-giving and life-enriching for those enduring it and for society?

From these questions I went on to explore three kinds of poverty and their relationship to human growth: the way we respond to others' poverty; different types of voluntary poverty; and our ways of dealing with our own involuntary poverty. I described sudden poverty as the simplest form and as quite distinct from the "never-having-had" experience. Catastrophes of various kinds bring "sudden poverty," and historically societies have imposed certain responses to it, such as almsgiving and hospitality, that help preserve the humanity of those with resources to help. Not to do so triggers guilt, but at the same time, I pointed out, a person must exercise careful discernment in determining which persons would benefit from caring intervention and one's own capability of meeting their needs. Through engagement in this form of discernment, we can grow in self-knowledge and compassion.

The enduring form of poverty afflicts whole regions and classes of society. Because it stunts every kind of growth, this kind is often self-perpetuating and as such, I wrote, is much harder to deal with than sudden poverty. When the privileged come to the realization of how they benefit from the permanent poverty of others, many demands emerge for them. Not only must they encounter the loss of their own self-esteem because of their involvement in enduring poverty, but they must also confront the very difficult questions concerning its fullest impact on all human growth and community.

I suggested voluntary poverty as a way to find some understanding of these issues. This ranges from moderating one's consumption to identifying completely with the seriously deprived in our society. To share with others in different ways can bring moderation and personal growth. To illustrate the nature of creative voluntary poverty, I cited the early Franciscans, Mother Teresa, and Dorothy Day, emphasizing at the same time that this kind of choice has always been limited to a few whose own life experience has brought them the courage and wholeness needed to live creatively and transcend the negative effects of sacrifice.

With the permanently poor, the response is often despair and apathy, although in some cases revolt leads to creative leadership that sets forth ways of transcending the poverty. In some way, we all know personal poverty, perhaps through illness, accident or various external circumstances we may experience either as a limitation or as a challenge to be worked around. Bereavement, no matter what its form, diminishes us, and it can either isolate us or thrust us into new depths of understanding and feeling for others in need, a growth-producing response. Any experience of drastic poverty can be the catalyst for self-transcendence, and we have many myths and legends from different cultures expressing that reality. Out of this recognition that some few individuals do transcend poverty, no matter how profound, and are transformed by it, may have come the traditional connection between poverty and a special blessedness. The beatitude may refer to the humility and courage that enable us to face our weakness, whatever its nature, and change. Without that, we do not grow.

Once my work at Union was completed, I returned to Africa, at the request of the Bishop of Liberia, Dillard Brown, to take over the headship of a school at Cape Palmas—Bishop Ferguson High School, where Cecily Delafield had been head. I was very happy to take up my work again, but with a different tribe, the Grebo, as well as with many non-tribal students. I was alone again, as I had no other religious with me, and there was only one other American on the staff of that school.

I spent a year and a half there, a fantastic experience. The school was in total disarray. There had been an interim principal between Cecily and me who apparently kept no records, neither financial nor academic, for I could not find any at all. There was a jumble of stuff in the files, and every now and then I would come upon a check that had not been cashed, so I had to start everything from scratch.

The boys' dormitory was smashed in, windows and doors broken, so that the boys could get out at night and go where they pleased. The chief of police came to see me one day and told me, "If I see your boys in town after dark, I'm going to lock them up for their protection." My response was to say, "Thank you very much." I had learned that Cape Palmas was notorious for its ritual murder society (like those operating under the surface in many parts of Africa). Kidnapping and an agonizing, painful form of death are the fate of its victims. I was not afraid for myself, because I knew that in their eyes I had no power since I was white, but I was terribly afraid for the students. We finally found enough money to repair the windows and doors of the dormitory and securely confine the boys at night. After putting one of the teachers to live with them there, I felt better.

I found that, for some reason, I was more successful in dealing with the boys than with the girls. I could be quite frank with the boys, but the girls seemed very withdrawn, not open to me, and I did not understand them. The faculty had at its head a fine young Nigerian, Jonathan Onabiyi, who was my assistant and my loyal helper during the whole time of my tenure there. It was an agonizing time.

One of the first jams I got into concerned a ward of President Tubman, a boy who had been totally defiant to the school authorities before I arrived. He lived in the dormitory but never went to class or to chapel. He was caught at a night club after hours and brought back to campus by the school's dean. When the faculty tried to discipline him, he denied having been there, and had the police arrest our dean. Because the president was away, I could do nothing until he returned to the country, but I realized that this was a real test of my authority and of my ability to run the school. I had talked to the boy and appealed to his pride in his family name to no avail. I told him, "I'm going to take you in to your guardian, Senator Gibson. I cannot keep you in school."

When the president returned, I awaited his reaction. I shall never forget the day that the presidential car drove up to the school grounds. A messenger, carrying a lime green envelope addressed to me, leapt out of the car. Onabiyi was with me. Like all the staff, he knew that President Tubman used lime green for his personal stationery. We read it together. It was a fine letter that said, "I don't want you to make any exception for Alexander because he is my son." We read that far and then Onabiyi and I danced a jig in celebration. "We're free! We've made it!" I knew then I wasn't going to be packed up and sent home.

My new adventures seemed to be marked by traumatic events, and another was in store. Bishop Dillard Brown, who had invited me to do the work in Cape Palmas, paid us a visit and celebrated the Eucharist for the school. He then went back to Monrovia on business and was murdered in his office, along with his treasurer. Both were shot at point blank. The assailant was known, for the secretary, who was also shot, survived and named him. After the news of Bishop Brown's death reached us, I went to Monrovia at once to take part in the wake and the funeral and see what help I could be. It was a terrible time. Why had the Bishop been murdered? Where was the murderer? What was going to happen next? Until George Brown was elected as Bishop Dillard Brown's successor, there was a difficult interim filled by Bishop Voegli, retired from Haiti. For the first time in its history, the Liberian police used a shortwave radio to try to hunt down a criminal. He was eventually captured, and after a good many years of dilly-dallying, and President Tubman's death, was executed for murder.

I continued to struggle at the school, trying to improve its religious instruction courses, solve its problems, set up financial and academic records, and work with some of the individual students. Although I made little progress in my efforts to straighten out affairs at the school in Las Palmas, I did make some enduring friendships, with Fr. Vaani Gray and his wife, Olive, and with my head prefect, Christopher Himie Davies. They were supportive no matter what happened.

Christopher once took me on a visit to his former village, Fishtown, where his chief lived. He told me ahead of time that the chief's house was not open to anybody who was not a member of the tribe, and that I would not be invited in, but I could look in the door. He took me to the door and, lo and behold, the chief came out and invited me in! I sat on one of the big chests in the reception room of the house where the black monkey skin, the symbol of his authority, was kept. Later I was told that a history of the Grebo tribe and a translation of the Bible into Grebo (or parts of it) were kept in that chest. After we left, I said to Christopher, "I thought you said I couldn't go in." He replied, "Oh, the chief is a Christian, and because you are a Christian, he could invite you in."

During my time at the school I experienced some real struggles with the student body. One of the really popular teachers, the soccer coach, was not loyal to me and stirred up the students against me. They began leaving me little threatening messages on my screen door because they wanted me to do something or other about soccer. In the end it was Christopher who settled the matter. As head prefect, he marched up to the school, taking those little notes with him, called the school together and said, "It is not good for Sr. Rachel that you speak to her in this way. You will make her sick. You may not do it. If you have complaints, bring them to me, and I will deal with them. If I think they should go to Sr. Rachel, I will take them. What are your complaints?" Someone said, "We don't get enough to eat." Christopher replied, "I have been here five years. They have put nothing more there, and they have taken nothing away. Tell me the next complaint." And so on, down through the list. He then came back and reported the whole thing to me. I knew, however, that my days at Cape Palmas were numbered and welcomed an invitation to return to Bolahun.

Towards the end of my first stay in Bolahun, Connor Lynn and I had begun to work on a plan for turning more authority over to Liberians. We did some workshops with the consultative council we had established, comprised of the town chief and elders and all the department heads, and it formally requested that I be returned to the mission to work with them. This was not a very popular suggestion at West Park, the Order's headquarters, because at Holy Cross I was regarded as somewhat of a firebrand, I think, by many who wanted to preserve the old ways. But in the end, having agreed that the council might choose whom they wanted, I was allowed to go.

The return trip to Bolahun was memorable. The little plane that took me back from Cape Palmas to Monrovia was jammed. I thought my pelvis would break as I was pushed into the back seat with two big men, a crate of hens behind me, but nothing would have made me stay over for another plane. I landed in Monrovia exhausted and needed several days of staying quiet and resting in the home of one of the A.I.D. people I knew. Eventually I got myself back to Bolahun, where I began the last months of my appointed time as a missionary.

Sr. Cornelia Ransom and I were there together for a while, working with Holy Cross to begin the process of turning over the administration of the mission to Liberians. I was also teaching religion in the high school, a source of real enjoyment. In an experiment with the seniors, I made a chart showing three streams: Christian, country religion, and Muslim. Every time I introduced a concept such as Christian belief about God, I also tried to find out from the students what the country people and the Moli (Muslim) people believed about God, in order to compare these with Christian teaching. This process led to a great deal of interesting discussion in religion classes.

We also had a whole series of workshops trying to prepare the people for handing over authority to the Liberians. Native rule was the cry of the day. It was in the air, especially among students, and there was also a great deal of violence and unrest throughout Africa. The crisis hit us in an unexpected way.

One fateful evening two or three children came up from the girls' boarding compound, demanding rice. They had had rice at their noon meal, the more substantial meal, so their demand was inappropriate. When Sr. Cornelia refused their request, they went back down to the girls' compound. Soon, surging up from the compound, came students throwing small stones and pebbles, which rattled on the roof. Eventually Cornelia decided to go for help. She could not go down the front walk because it was filled with protesting students, but she did manage to get out the back way to the hospital and bring one of the hospital workers to our assistance.

At the same time the boys' compound began revolting. They raided the office of the principal, an African like themselves, dumped the school duplicator in the swamp, and generally raised cain. In the end, students on the girls' compound did the same thing, smashing up light bulbs and robbing the storehouse. The school authorities called an emergency meeting of everybody concerned and suspended all the resisting students for two weeks. They jeered as they left by bus for their homes. That was the end of that.

In the aftermath I received word from my family that my mother was dying and that if I wanted to see her, I had better come at once. My contract with the Episcopal Church headquarters had already expired, and I was sixty-five years old, not eligible for reappointment. So I left Africa with sadness, but despite all the traumas, with a deep love for the people and a great hope for their future.

New and Different Ministries

I returned from Africa in 1971 for what turned out to be my last visit with my mother, who was very frail. She died suddenly in hospital after a hemorrhage. She was buried from the parish church in Sharon and laid to rest in her family's plot in Thomaston, Maine. Her death was the most radical bereavement of my life.

After the funeral I returned to Vails Gate. Not too long after that I moved on to my next job, which was to assist a priest, William Noble, at a small mission he ran on the campus of Georgia Southern College in Statesboro. He was looking for an assistant to help him with his work with Episcopal students. Sr. Andrea, then our superior, suggested the possibility of my taking it on. I was glad to go. There I was lodged with a Roman Catholic sister from Glenmary who was working with students of her church.

Georgia Southern College was part of the white establishment in Statesboro, symbolized by both the layout and the architecture of the town. The town center was inhabited by whites, the courthouse was white, and the paved roads did not run beyond the edge of the white residential district. Once you left that district and moved into the part of Statesboro where black people lived, there was neither running water nor paved roads.

In the 1970s universities in the South were faced with the necessity of doing something about integration, and to comply with the law the college put one black person in the lowest staff position of the Department of Continuing Education. No courses in black studies were offered, in spite of the fact that the graduates of the School of Education who went into teaching in Georgia would have to face racially mixed classes for the first time in their lives. The reality of this seemed to have been repressed. Education courses were not revised to meet the new situation, and no effort was made to understand either African-American culture or the kind of stress integrated classes would create for children of both races.

I decided to offer a course that would undertake to do both. Since I could not get it into the regular curriculum, I offered it through the Department of Education by Extension and worked with Junius Reed, the one black person on the college faculty. We planned a series of eight evenings with a group from the black community in Statesboro, including the churches, and designed a survey of African-American and African culture (a big thing to tackle). Since this was before very much had been done on black studies in this country, there was not a great deal of information available to us. A few professors helped Junius and me in carrying out the program: the professor of political science did a presentation one evening on African political history and government, the professor of music offered a program of African music, and on still another evening an English professor gave some readings from African poetry. For the remaining evenings in the course we relied on movies and discussions.

One of the films, *A Man Called Charlie*, was the story of perhaps the only person then still alive who had been brought to this country as a slave. I had previewed it with Jim Mincie, a black student who for quite a while had been refused admission to the campus because he was said to be an agitator. As we sat watching the movie in the back of the auditorium Trinity Church also used for its services, I noticed that he was doubled up in grief. At the end he said, "Sister, how can your people have done this to my people? How can we believe, how can we be Christians together?" It was a terrible moment. I could do nothing except sit there, listening to him, holding him. Somehow in the silence we arrived at a mutual acceptance that enabled us to move on and plan the rest of the course. Jim was able to lead some of the discussions, something he did very well, and at the end of the series, he embraced me before the entire audience.

Another of our undertakings there was what we called a Taizé weekend. We invited two of the Taizé brothers who were stationed in Atlanta to come and work with groups of students, both white and black, to pray with us, share in our discussions, and lead the night watch. Students came from other campuses in the state as well. One of the things that most impressed some of the white students was the way in which the Taizé brothers began their prayers with silence, a long silence into which we were all drawn. The weekend was held in the midst of enormous tension, for you could almost cut the atmosphere with a knife in Statesboro during those days. Despite this, I would say that the weekend was a great success and quite an experience for Trinity, for it was the first time such a racially mixed group had been entertained, fed, and lodged there in the mission building.

After my term at Statesboro was over, I went to the convent at Augusta for our annual chapter. After some painful and fruitless discussion about where I should be stationed, Sr. Alice offered to take me as part of the group that also included Srs. Marianne and Columba to open a small house in Manhattan at Calvary Church. The four of us were to work on the staff of Calvary with the rector, Tom Pike, and Steve Garmey. We had parts of two floors of Calvary House, but for our meals we had to use the big kitchen in the basement that was shared by the whole parish. For the most part, we said the daily office in the church or the side chapel. During the time I was stationed there (1972-74), I was program director, and I learned a great deal from working with the different groups who wanted to use Calvary's space. Some floors of Calvary House were given over to a program for mentally retarded children; the auditorium was often used by groups such as Alcoholics Anonymous. Various theater groups often applied to use the Little Theater or the church itself. It was my job to schedule all of these and to make some decisions about what we could sponsor and what we could not. It was not an easy job, but an interesting one.

At that same time I found a job through a Moravian friend who had been teaching at the Baptist Educational Center in Harlem. The program, sponsored by Union Theological Seminary, was aimed at updating Black baptist ministers who had little formal education. When I went to talk to the seminary's dean about it, I had to persuade him to take on a white person. By 1972, Black people had distanced themselves from whites. I told the dean that I was home from Africa and tired of all these white faces; I wanted to work again with Blacks. I also told him about the farewell banquet just before I left Bolahun, where the chief stated that I had lived out the promises made to them at my arrival—to share anything helpful from my past experience, to forego telling them what to do with their children, and to be open to discussion. I think my recalling that story helped the dean to overcome his reluctance to take on a white person. Anyhow, I got the job.

Twice a week I went up to Harlem on the subway, lugging my pack of heavy books, notebooks, and course notes. I taught English and Old Testament to classes of eight to twelve adults, some of whom had only a fifth-grade education. But all of them showed a deep love for Scripture and the church. They had little acquaintance with the whole Bible, but what they knew, they knew well and loved well.

As usual, I set out to create my own course and devised a time line showing the different watersheds in the history of the people of God. Within that time line I put the different books of the Bible. It was quite a shock for them to realize that Genesis was not the first book to be written, but rather that it was written at different periods in history, some quite late. All through their studies they were confronted with the very puzzling fact that the Bible does not begin with Genesis and go in a straight line to Revelation.

I loved my work and the people there at the Baptist Educational Center. The students, mostly ministers—some in small store front operations and others in larger parishes—had to work fulltime at other jobs to keep their families going. One was a diamond factory guard, another a barber, still another a bus driver. They were also interested in perfecting their English skills to help in keeping up with their children, whose education had started moving beyond their own. One of the women students told me that the two things she feared most for her children were the drug merchants who came on the school grounds with spiked Cokes to entice their children, and the Black Muslims who attacked their faith as Christians. I liked and respected these adult students, for they were very devout, unfailingly kind, humorous, generous, and loyal.

Every day we ate together a wonderful meal brought in by women who helped at the center. It was a merry time! Then I would toil home again, my arms full of heavy books. I will never forget getting on the subway one day when it was very crowded and I was very tired. Sighting an empty seat way down the other end of the car, I went to it and sat down. The woman beside me said, "I *hoped* you'd see this seat." I felt very comfortable on those subways taking me back and forth to Harlem. I cherish the fact that at my ordination, both as deacon and as priest, delegations were present from the Baptist Educational Center. Towards the end of my time there, the dean said, "When you first came, we didn't know how it was going to work. Now we know that we love you." That was a real tribute I value to this day.

In 1974 I moved to the General Theological Seminary to work on my S.T.M. degree in preparation for ordination to the diaconate. The move came about partly through a meeting with Alan Jones, a professor at the seminary, at a party with the Sisters of the Holy Spirit. There Alan approached me, told me who he was, and said, "I've heard about your community and would like to know more about you." I said, "Well, I'll tell you more about us, but you won't like it!" He was furious! He asked me how I knew what he thought while pursuing me around the room. I invited him to come and celebrate the Eucharist for us one evening and talk with us afterwards. He became one of our friends, though never an uncritical one.

Eventually I moved from Calvary House and went to live in a little apartment at the back of the Jones's apartment at General Seminary where I continued my theological studies. I spent several happy years with the Jones family, learning, among many other things, about what it means to be a mother. As I watched Josephine Jones with her two little girls, I became very aware of the responsibility of being a mother, and of her total and complete dedication to her small children, the extent of her self-giving without any possibility of putting her own needs first. I also learned something about discipline. Josephine was patient and loving and explained things to the girls, but when enough was enough, they knew it. She would say, "Now I've told you what I want you to do, and I want you to do it and no more talk about it. All right...one, two." I never heard "three" because by then they had fled and gone to do what she asked.

At the same time that I began my work for an S.T.M., I began working with Alan Jones on the new Center for Christian Spirituality, which he was in the process of establishing. Its purpose was to foster the serious study of spirituality and spiritual direction at the seminary. Courses were added to the curriculum to enable students to obtain a graduate degree in spiritual direction. We also brought in outside speakers for the whole seminary community; sometimes Alan would invite just one to do a presentation, at other times there would be several speakers talking with each other. After that a panel might take over, do some questioning, carry on more discussion, and then open it to the audience. I mounted the academic ladder, becoming first a tutor, then a lecturer, and finally an assistant professor.

My movement into the discipline of Christian spirituality was influenced in some ways by a friendship begun in Liberia. I first met Lucerne Montague when I was stationed at Bolahun. She was working in Monrovia with the literacy program sponsored by Koinonia, a residential community near Baltimore. Lucerne had come up to Bolahun to spend time in retreat and prayer with us, and we stayed in touch after each of us returned to this country. Although she was a faithful member of the Baptist Church, she disagreed with a great many of their teachings. She also loved both Quaker silence and the Anglican liturgy, especially the Eucharist, but somehow she managed to keep her own integrity without confusion.

When I was at Union Seminary, Lucerne was at Columbia. Since we both needed some time off once a week, we decided to take Saturdays together. No books were to be opened for study at those times. We used to meet for a late breakfast, have some time reading Scripture, ponder it in silence, then share what it meant to us and pray about it. Lucerne was a lot better at this extemporaneous prayer than I was; usually when I was faced with a request to pray out loud, I would begin, "Direct us, O Lord, with thy most gracious favor..."! But little by little, with her encouragement, I ventured out. It is through Lucerne that I received the gift of being able to pray freely out loud with other people. This has been very helpful to me in my work in spiritual direction.

After that we would spend the rest of the day going together to see or do something different, pleasant, stimulating. Since neither of us had very much money, most of the things we chose were free—galleries, a street fair, or a carnival were frequent choices. Once we walked all the way down to Chinatown, one of our many walks through the streets of New York. These Saturdays were pleasant intervals in a terribly busy and pressured time for both of us.

After I went to General, we stayed in touch. By that time Lucerne was interested in learning about music and practicing music therapy. She asked me if I would be willing to be a guinea pig. Knowing her faith and her integrity, I trusted Lucerne, and so I said, "Sure." She would lay out some blankets and pillows on the floor, stretch me out flat on them, bind up my eyes so that I was not able to see anything, and then put earphones on me. She controlled the music that I heard, music that blotted out everything else. Then she would ask me to tell her what images I saw.

I remember once seeing a beach and a pair of empty rubber boots that I thought belonged to my father. Another time, when I saw my grandmother in a rocking chair, the picture was inside a tear. Lucerne used different kinds of music to get different kinds of images out of me; one particular experience was very dark and aggressive. I was being driven at great speed across a black bridge in the darkness, a bridge with no sides. Little flames took the place of railings. Another time she took me down inside the horn of a unicorn; I went down inside of it—down, down, down. At the bottom I was aware of an opening out and of clear crystal water, braided as it flowed over the golden sandy bottom of pebbles. Then I was brought up, up, up towards the light, which widened into a circular opening fringed with grass and flowers into which shone the full face of the sun—a wonderful experience.

Another image I came up with was of a tree, a beautiful tree with all its roots and fruits and creatures. Sometimes after one of these sessions she would ask me to draw a mandala, recording in color what I had seen. I think that all of this experience loosened me up, helped me to come more in touch with my own interior, a place where the little tear-stained child lived. What I learned later about imaging in prayer and also about imagelessness was also grounded in those times with Lucerne.

My ordination to the diaconate is another story. In 1975 I went to a meeting at Union Theological Seminary to address the question of whether or not women should be ordained to the priesthood. The discussion included a paper by the New Testament scholar Reginald Fuller, in which he concluded that there was nothing in the New Testament that would prevent women from being ordained. That was enough for me. He had been my teacher at Union some years before, and I respected his scholarship. I decided then that it was important for me to support the ordination of women. It had not yet occurred to me that I needed to pursue ordination myself; I had a ministry already and was happy in it. However, at that same meeting, one of the women addressed me, "You are a member of one of the most radical of women's orders. How would your community feel if some of you became ordained as deacons? It would be helpful to the movement as a whole because religious in our church are greatly respected."

Except for one incident at Calvary Church, I had not thought of ordination for myself, although I was sure that the time had come when the church had to speak to the world through both sexes, in the pulpit and at the altar. It was Tom Pike who clarified it for me. As he watched me one day clearing away the altar vessels after the Eucharist, he said, "When I see you handle those vessels, I think, 'You ought to be a priest!' Have you ever thought about it?" I was slow in taking this in. My first step was in response to the woman at Union. When I took the matter to our chapter at Vails Gate that year, I discovered that Columba Gillis and Mary Michael Simpson were moving in that same direction. We asked for and received permission to go forward for ordination to the diaconate, with the understanding that if the Episcopal Church acted favorably on the ordination of women to the priesthood at the next General Convention, we would also be free to seek ordination as priests.

The three of us were to be ordained to the diaconate together that year at the Cathedral of St. John the Divine in Manhattan, and I asked my brother Dick to be my lay presenter at the ordination. I wanted, for once in my life, to have somebody from my own family take part in my ministry, my Christian vocation. I realized that even though they could not participate within the context of religious life, which they did not understand at all, perhaps they could do it here.

I remember that when we were discussing it, Dick gave me a quizzical look and said, "Lib, it's controversial, isn't it?" hoping it was. I said, "Yes, indeed it is." He was going over the service, looking at what he would have to do as my presenter. At that time, 1975, the service required the bishop to ask the presenters, "Are they worthy?" When Dick came to this and saw the reply was "They are worthy," he looked at me and said, "Lib, how do I know you're worthy?" I said, "OK, you can read my exams if you want to!" I fished them out and gave them to him. At the service itself, he stood behind me, and when that point in the liturgy came, I heard that little note of amusement and irony in his voice as he said, "They are worthy."

At the end of the school year, when I was completing my course work at General, I found myself at a loose end. My course work for the S.T.M. was finished and the next year was to be spent working on my thesis, a survey of attitudes to poverty from Clement of Alexandria to Benedict, to help me in my search for a new understanding of monastic poverty as simplicity of life and community of goods. I woke up one night in my bed at the Jones's apartment asking, "Where am I going to go next year, Lord?" And the Lord said, "Well, you can go to Grandchamp." So I did, and it was a wonderful choice.

My Year at Grandchamp

*I*n the summer of 1975, I traveled to Europe with Muriel Anne Hutchinson, a former teacher at Margaret Hall School, on my way to the community of Grandchamp. After landing in Germany, we went south, stopping in Immhausen, Strasbourg, and then Colmar, the site of one of the most memorable of my impressions. There we went first to see the old town, then the Romanesque Dominican church with its lovely choir, its fine lines not much obscured by Baroque choir stalls. In the middle of the choir, at its entrance, is the *Madonna of the Rose Bush* by Schoengauer. The picture stands alone in its graceful shrine, a thing so beautiful it took me by the throat. The rose red of the Virgin's robe, the blue angels above her wide, serene, intelligent forehead, her fine hands and the lively child formed a harmonious, luminous whole. The church provides a perfect setting for the painting. The windows are either grisaille or colored with the rich deep blues and reds of the finest medieval glass. The slender columns of rose-red stone define the shape of the early Gothic shell of the church and run into the ribs of the vaulting without the break of capitals.

When we went back the next morning to sit again before the Virgin's picture, I thought of all the Blessed Virgin Mary has meant in Christian history. This Mary of Colmar is no second-rate person. She is absolutely primary, full of dignity, grace, and a peaceful inward balance and joy. She is surrounded by roses on a trellis with carved and painted angels and musical instruments on the inner frame of the shrine; the light crown is over her head, not on it. It is a place full of power and light and glowing with beauty. I thought of Frau Vera from the community at Imshausen and her strong beliefs about the place of women in the church. Much as I disagreed with her position that women must leave leadership and priesthood to men, I did feel that the Schoengauer Virgin spoke to us of feminine grace and power much as Frau Vera would speak.

From Colmar we went to Basel, where we stayed that night at a tiny hotel near the station. We went twice to the Kunstmuseum and saw paintings by Holbein, Cranach, Breugel, and El Greco, but to me nothing was as memorable as Holbein's portrait of Erasmus and his panel of the Dead Christ. We also saw a fine exhibition of Kathe Kollwitz's lithographs.

We then took a night train through Zurich to Rome. Through some mistake in our travel arrangements, no one met us there, but we found our way finally to the Minerva Hotel near the Pantheon. The hotel was immense, palatial, and not very handsome, but we had a cheap and quite comfortable big room and bath. An evening tour of Rome gave me the impression of overripeness; everything is so heavy and rich from the gold of Europe poured into this city for a thousand years and more. I felt as if I were lost in an immense fruit cake! I think I also suffered a bit from culture shock, as well as being tired, hungry, and confused by the currency. We seemed to be spending millions!

We walked to and around the Forum, which was impressive, hot, full of fragments of pillars and foundations. So many broken stones—we could hardly figure out what had been where. The Arch of Titus and the Senate House, however, were recognizable, and I imagined Cicero going over his notes as he was carried in his litter on his way to the Forum. That evening we attended a performance of the opera *Aida* in the open air at the Baths of Caracalla.

The next day we went to St. Paul's-inside-the-Walls, the American church, for a 10:30 Eucharist. When the priest invited all who were ordained to help distribute the Eucharist and to concelebrate, a Dutch Reformed minister accepted the invitation. The church is modern, built in the late nineteenth or early twentieth century, Romanesque in style, with Burne-Jones mosaics and J.P. Morgan's face on St. Ambrose! (Morgan, it seems, was one of its benefactors.)

The next day we set out, guidebook in hand, to go to the Coliseum where the martyrs' blood was shed. We saw the spot where the Colossus of Nero was located and tried to realize a little of what martyrdom meant for those early Christians. After this we returned to the Forum and spent more time in the House of the Vestals.

I wondered how these women passed their thirty years of celibate service to the state—were they so limited in their education and consciousness that they were content with their lot, which was to be carried about and to do a few duties in the Temple of Vesta? Did they pray together, sing or dance, play games, sew, embroider? Did they enjoy making the consuls wait for them—one of their privileges—and crossing the path of criminals whom they could pardon or refuse to pardon? Were they envious or jealous of each other? Did the Pontifex Maximus have to settle their palavers? How did the littlest ones manage, who were taken around the age of ten? Were the older ones loving with them? What instinct is it in the human race that produces eunuchs, high priests, vestal virgins, and the monastic life? Is it for the tribe, for the city, for the people of God? Taboo and sacrifice, sacrality and power—what are their meanings?

In the afternoon we set out for the Church of St. John Lateran and, by mistakenly getting off the bus much too soon, we saw St. Clement's Basilica as a reward. This church of Constantine, remade on top of an earlier one, has a lovely, simple altar on top of a pagan temple of the god Mithras. This beautiful basilica church with its stone choir and ambos is now used by the Irish Dominicans. On the bus home a beautiful young woman gave me her seat, and another gave hers to an old man. Perhaps they were Christians?

The most closed-in faces I saw were those of so many of the priests and the nuns. They seemed shut into their own world and unrelated to those around them, moving about in habits made of serge in the hot weather, July in Rome. One night our square was filled with billowing nuns in white habits, wimples, and black mantles; most of them were fat. They seemed a race apart, spoke only to each other, and moved in waves. On the other hand, I saw a young girl with a frightened, wistful face talking with a Franciscan in the aisle of St. John Lateran. As I noticed them, I thought his whole stance was attentive, quiet, concerned, brotherly, and priestly.

Then I found myself wondering, "Where is Pope John XXIII in all this vast, over-rich chocolate cake of a church? Where is the pure spirit of the early martyrs, of the great fathers of the western church—Augustine, Ambrose, and Gregory? Where is Catherine of Genoa, and where is the austere Catherine of Siena, who is represented in plaster, sweet and plump, crowned and bejeweled under the altar of the Church of Santa Maria della Minerva? And where are the Christians? Are they the folks swarming to the Basilica for an indulgence, reciting rosaries in side chapels, buying medals and pious images?" The two girls on the bus and the Franciscan friar were for me the visible signs of Christ.

Another day we went to St. Peter's to see the Pietà, which is on the right as you enter Michelangelo's maimed basilica. Almost everything he did was ruined by someone, sometimes by himself. This one was marred by the extension of the nave from a Greek to a Latin cross, making it impossible to see the dome from the front entrance. In comparison with everything else at St. Peter's, the Pietà is small; above it is a plain cross, below it a simple altar. Since the attack a few years ago by a demented man with an axe, the statue has been protected by a glass screen.

Like the Schoengauer Virgin, the Pietà was one of the most beautiful objects I had ever seen. It made me cry; it gave me goose pimples. How could anyone carve such a thing? The body of Jesus is so beautiful, utterly relaxed in death in its every part. It reminds me of Adam in the Sistine Chapel, yet it is wholly different, for it is the body of a man with mature muscles, complete in its development and deprived of life. Adam is just opening to life, untried life. Mary is a throne, a mother, a mourner, and an offerer. The whole composition with its perfection of line and complementarity is very moving. We looked and looked, walked about briefly, saw the St. Peter statue with its worn toe (we had no desire to touch it), and the Great Altar beyond. We prayed there for the Pope, the Roman Church, and for all Christian people, "that we might be one, that the world might believe."

From Rome we went to Florence. In my notes I wrote: "An incredible city, golden, light, open, compared to rich and heavy Rome." We saw the Baptistry where Michelangelo and Dante had been baptized, with its golden doors by Ghiberti, and the Duomo with another Pietà by Michelangelo done in his old age, showing Nicodemus with the body of Jesus. Nicodemus is Michelangelo himself; the figure embodies his own experience of mourning. As the Last Judgment seems to express his rage and frustration, so the Pietà expresses Michelangelo's sadness, his resignation, and his transcendence of the human limitations, the interference, and stony-heartednesses he encountered in his lifetime.

Our trip by train from Florence to Geneva afforded us a glorious view of the Alps. After spending a few days in Geneva, we proceeded to Neuchatel, where one of the sisters met us and drove us to Grandchamp. Muriel stayed with me a few days before her return to the United States, and I then moved into a small room in Amandier, one of the big houses in the group of buildings that house the community. I described the room and my initial feelings in my journal: "It has nice old board panels, a comfortable bed, but little room for working or for my winter clothes. There is much silence in a brisk, hard-working community whose rapid French I cannot understand much of. I think I am in for culture shock."

I was quite unhappy my first weeks at Grandchamp. I had little contact with other guests, most of whom spoke French or German, and at first I had little contact with the religious either. This was chiefly because I arrived at the time of their annual meeting, or *conseil*, when they were much occupied with their own affairs. I felt very much cut off, lonely, and frustrated.

At this time I had a dream I think was helpful to me, a dream of a big crystal container, half full of water, in which floated a twig with a few leaves on it. On them perched a bird, alive, with a bright eye looking at me. I think it was an image of myself, cut off, alone, unable to reach anybody, and yet still alive, still determined to live, to make it. One of the young women who was working at Grandchamp as an aide soon realized that I was depressed and lonely. In talking with me, she drew out of me how I felt. When I was tempted to give up and go home, she encouraged me to see it through by saying, "In the end, when you leave Grandchamp, you'll cry."

Part of my trouble at first was not knowing enough French. I can read French easily and I can speak it when I can get my mind on it, but it is very hard for me to hear it when it is spoken too quickly. At the beginning of my stay, some lessons with Soeur Marguerite Françoise helped me. One thing she told me was, "When you start a conversation in a shop or an office, say to them, '*Je parle français un peu.*'" That was a very good piece of advice; it put them on the alert that here was a person who knew only a little French and for whom the language must be spoken simply and slowly. Having Soeur Maria as my *vis-à-vis*, that is to say, the official link between me and the community, also helped me a great deal. I was allowed to join a *foyer*, one of the groups into which the community is divided and which meet regularly every Saturday afternoon for *révision de vie*. This is a time of mutual reflection and response, either to verses from the rule or from Scripture. In this kind of group reflection one does not argue with other people, nor does anyone tell another person what to do. We listened to one another, and in this way came to know a little of the work of God in one another and express some of our aspirations and problems. I found it a wonderfully helpful experience, even when I could not understand all of it.

My thesis on poverty went slowly but steadily. To help me in my research, I was introduced to the librarian of the *Bibliothèque des Pasteurs* in Neuchatel. Neuchatel is a Protestant canton, and the city has a Protestant theological library, a very fine one with plenty of editions of the church fathers, mostly in French, the language I used for most of my research in Switzerland. When I needed something from Roman Catholic writings, mostly from the Middle Ages, I went to Fribourg, stayed with the Dominicans there, and used the university library. I soon learned to get along alone on trains and trams (there are not very many buses) and do the business I needed to do—buy the ticket, ask for times, and all that sort of thing. I felt much better as I became freer and more able to operate on my own.

I especially remember Palm Sunday that year. Large, blown-up photographs of people's faces—children, old men, young men, women, some alone in a picture, some pictured with one or two others—were placed around the edge of the chapel or leaned up against the altar. At the time of the homily, we were invited to choose a picture and have a conversation with it, talking about what Palm Sunday meant to us and what it might mean to the person in the picture. I chose a picture of an older man, an African, but not in African dress. I figured he must be South African; something about the sadness of his face made me think that, and I spoke to him about his own situation and about mine. "*Sors du tombeau!*" I heard, and then I heard him say in reply, "*Seigneur, comment et Seigneur, quand?*" "Lord, *when* and Lord, *how?* When is salvation coming to us black people in South Africa and how can it come? What is the possibility for me of freedom and of a full life?" I sat on the edge of my pew trying to keep my mouth shut as other people shared what they had experienced in their conversation with their picture. I was afraid I would make mistakes in French. But suddenly it came right out of my mouth. "*Sors du tombeau!*" "*Seigneur, comment et Seigneur, quand?*"

Another memorable occasion for me during Holy Week was the *Grand Pardon*. It is something like our Maundy Thursday remembrance when we wash one another's feet, but this occurred on Wednesday and was a preparation for the Triduum. It was very simple. There were some prayers and psalms at the beginning, and then the Superior, Soeur Minke, (whose title in French is *Soeur Responsable*) knelt down before each sister and said, "*Ma soeur, pardonne-moi.*" The sister raised her up and said, "*Je te pardonne.*" She went on to each one of us in this way; then we went to one another. I was allowed to be present at this, Soeur Minke said, because I had lived with them for nearly a year. It was a wonderful way to begin the deepening experience of the liturgy of the last three days of Holy Week.

Also during my time there, sometime in the spring, we commemorated the death of Dietrich Bonhoeffer. I had been reading Eberhard Bethge's life of Bonhoeffer, in which he spoke of Bonhoeffer going "naked under the tender leaves of spring, down the shallow steps to the gallows." I had not realized the Nazis stripped their victims naked before they hanged them.

On the Feast of the Transfiguration, the 6th of August, we had a very special celebration. We arose early to say the Night Office, had some time in silent prayer, and went very early to the refectory for a bowl of coffee and some bread. Then we started to walk, two by two, stopping every once in a while to recite a psalm or sing a hymn. As we plunged through some woods and down around the bottom of a field, Soeur Minke pointed to the rising wooded land on the other side and said, "That's where we're going, up there." We entered the woods and walked some way in an ascending path. Suddenly we came out upon a ledge that faced a great ravine. In one direction we could see the lake, and in the other a little village. Facing us was another ledge like our own, looming up like the prow of a ship. We sat there on that wide stone ledge and listened to the Gospel of the Transfiguration. After that each of us was invited to reflect on the meaning for us of the Transfiguration, each in his or her own language. For me the Transfiguration was the anniversary of Hiroshima, the very opposite of transfiguration—disfiguration on a grand scale—so I spoke about that. After each person who spoke a different language put in his or her own part (for the guests were both men and women), the sisters broke out a little bread and chocolate from their pockets for us to eat before we started back down.

Another important experience for me came when I was praying in L'Arche, the big chapel made out of an old dyers' shed. The inside walls are brown-stained boards. Here and there on two sides of the interior are little openings filled with panes of colored glass—very beautiful, very harmonious. The chapel itself is separated from some rooms below used for guest rooms by a thick floor of cement that is muffled with rugs, rag rugs, so that one is quiet there. As I was praying there one day, I was thinking how safe it was and how I loved to be there, held up in worship in that silence. And then a little voice said to me, "Do you *really* want to be held in this deep silence all the time? Is this your future?" And I realized that deep down below there was something or someone I needed to hear. There was a little tear-stained child, frightened, disgruntled, discouraged. I asked her to come up and sit with me and share in my prayer and my praise, and I talked with her. In this, one of my most important life-changing experiences, I realized that simply to sit in the quiet on and on was not what I was called to do for the rest of my life, even though I was certainly called to have plenty of time for prayer and silence.

Grandchamp is silent most of the time. Only on Sunday afternoons is there an exception, during *révision de vie,* supper, and the washing of dishes. One can always speak with one's *vis à vis,* but aside from that the community observes contemplative silence and does its work in that quietness. I was much attracted, but I also realized again, as at Fairacres, that I was an American woman, and not a European, and that I needed not only to have silence, but also to be in touch with my own inner child and with the other people around me who would form my life when I returned home.

A great joy during all my time at Grandchamp was to be able to walk to the lake, up into the foothills of the Jura Mountains. Very often in the afternoons I spent hours walking, usually with a companion, for miles and miles in all directions. One of my favorite walks was to go up through a vineyard from which we could see the lake and sometimes the Alps, across the army shooting range and into a little village called Bole. Once I was stopped by an automobile full of people who wanted to know whether they were in Switzerland or France! Bole is in the foothills of the Juras, and of course just over the Juras is France. Other times we would walk down to the lake behind Grandchamp or in the other direction along the Areuse to Boudry or to Cortaillod, and then down to another spot on the lake.

I finished my thesis, sent it home in time for it to be read and accepted, and received my degree *in absentia*. Then came the time for me to go home. Just as the young woman had predicted during the early days of my time there, I wept when I left Grandchamp. When I went down to the courtyard to wait for transportation to the airport, I found the community gathered in a great circle to greet me and have a final prayer together. Remembering my contribution to the Palm Sunday liturgy, they gave me an icon of Jesus calling Lazarus out of the tomb, "*Sors du tombeau.*" "Come out of the tomb."

It is still in my room upstairs in the Manhattan convent, and its message to me has new meaning as I live through these days of chemotherapy when the forces of disease and the forces of healing meet in my body and in my spirit. When I find myself withdrawing into self-pity, discouragement, and apathy, I think of Jesus' voice calling to me, "Why are you in that grubby, dead place, with dead leaves, that cold, wet, clammy, deathly place? Come out into the light. *Sors du tombeau.*" This message, *Sors du tombeau*, joins me to the spirit of life and healing and hope.

Ordination to the Priesthood

On my return from Grandchamp in the fall of 1976, I went to live for another year with Alan Jones and his family at General Seminary. About that time I also became involved with the Community of Sarah and Abraham in Portland, Maine. This is an intentional community of men and women who meet together at the home of Nancy and Hank Beebe for prayer, reflection and dinner, followed by a lot of music in the evening. Hank and Nancy have a big house and big hearts; they have attracted many people from all walks of life and all kinds of religion—or none—to join them in this weekly meeting.

During my first years back at General they asked me to be chaplain to the group, and after my ordination to the priesthood in the winter of 1977, I used to go to Portland once a quarter to celebrate for them. I still have a much cherished link with that community. Hank Beebe wrote a joyous anthem dedicated to me for my ordination—"This is the day which the Lord has made"—and came down to play it. Barry Wood, whom I had met at Union Theological Seminary, had also belonged to the Community of Sarah and Abraham from the beginning. In those days he was doing his residency in psychiatry at Roosevelt Hospital as well as studying for a theological degree. Together we belonged to a group of Anglicans at Union that met Wednesdays after the Eucharist for breakfast and some time together with the Anglican faculty—John MacQuarrie and

Reginald Fuller. Barry moved to Portland from New York soon after the Beebes did, and those three were at the heart of the Community of Sarah and Abraham.

When Alan Jones went off on his sabbatical, he left me in charge of the Center for Christian Spirituality. Since this meant quite diverse and sometimes quite demanding responsibilities, Mary Coelho became my assistant. Before he left Alan had invited an Anglican priest called Peter Spink to come and speak on healing, and because of my leeriness on the whole subject of healing, I was anxious about meeting him. The day of his arrival, I was in the secretary's office, leaning over the desk, when I became aware of somebody behind me. When I turned around and saw Peter Spink standing there, his face so warm and open and loving, like a sunrise, I took to him at once. Peter had established a house of contemplative prayer for men and women, a residential community at Tunbridge Wells in Kent, England, and increasingly it was a place where East and West could meet in prayer. Whenever I was in England, I always took some time to visit Kent House, a place where I could touch down and feel at home.

Before going to Grandchamp, I had started the practice of sharing a "monastic breakfast" with a small group of seminarians. We used to meet in any old place in the West Building, a corner here, a table there, just two or three of us, and spend an hour early each day gathered in silence. After I moved to my own apartment in White Hall at the seminary, I could set up a full-scale breakfast with coffee and the makings of tea, granola and yogurt, bread, cheese, and fruit every day. People would bring their own spiritual reading or their journals. There were three rules—no talking, no smoking, no studying. Some people came every single morning, some less regularly but as often as possible; I do not remember a time when nobody came. It was the beginning of a custom I have kept up to this day. At the present time it is still going on every Thursday morning at General in Julian House, my office there, with students and often the Dean leading it.

While I was working at the Center, we had a retreat led by Tilden Edwards, the noted writer and spiritual director, at the retreat house of the Community of St. John Baptist in Mendham, New Jersey. That was my first experience of Tilden in that role and my relationship with him deepened because of it. When I asked him during the retreat to be my spiritual director, he responded by asking me why I wanted him. I said, "Because I think you can stand up to me!" That has proved to be very true, and I thank God for it.

Before my ordination to the priesthood, I went up to our mother house at Vails Gate to make my pre-ordination retreat. I had an experience there that is apparently common to many women at some point before their actual ordination to the priesthood. I was praying in the chapel when suddenly it seemed as if the place was filled with thunder, and a voice said to me, "Are *you* going up there behind that altar, you, a *woman*? You're going to stand up there and celebrate the Eucharist?" And it roared on and on and on like a thunderstorm, accusing and menacing. "Well," I said, looking towards the altar and thinking about it, "Yep, I am. I've gotten this far and I'm going to go through with it."

The next day dawned bright and lovely, and the voice had died completely away, never to return. Everything was open and inviting. My ordination day was a wonderful one, and I had the support of so many people. Barry Wood was the preacher and David Hurd the organist; he took over very graciously at the last moment, when the organist who had offered his services withdrew. My youngest brother John was the lay presenter, Alan Jones the clerical presenter. My brother Dick and his family were there and Josephine Jones with their newborn baby, Edward, in her arms. It was a special joy for me to have Tom Shaw of the Cowley Fathers at the service because of my relationship with the Society of St. John the Evangelist, which goes back to my teens, and the next morning to have him kneel and receive Holy Communion from me.

A delegation from the Baptist Educational Center in Harlem and Amos Bani Collins from Liberia also came to take part and support me on that day. After the ordination itself, when I came out into the seminary close, there were so many people waiting to greet me and kneel for my first priestly blessing—something I had not imagined! Among them was Steven Garmey, who pulled out of his pocket a beautiful little bronze crucifix from North Africa that I still have on my desk. I remember students and family and friends and faculty, all looking happy over this event. I was the first woman to be ordained in the Chapel of the Good Shepherd. At my first Eucharist the day after my ordination, I had Alan Jones, Boyce Bennett, professor of Old Testament, and Tommy Talley, professor of liturgics, in the sanctuary with me—Boyce on my left pointing out the places for me.

It should be said here that, despite considerable support from the student body for my ordination, there was also a very vocal group of people in opposition to it who mounted a vigil of protest during the service. They also came to see me and warned me of what a dreadful thing I was doing. This was the lot of all of us women ordinands in those days. Another expression of opposition was the letter from the ECM (Evangelical and Catholic Mission) telling me how sorry I would be if I did this dreadful thing. Of course it fell on deaf ears, and I went ahead with the ordination.

~

We've had our first "take me off your mailing list" response to the announcement in the newsletter about my coming ordination. In the same mail a supportive post card from a bishop. (To Charlotte Moore, February 9, 1977)

~

As I look back now over eleven years' experience as a priest, I am happy to be part of a growing assembly of ordained women. So many of them are highly competent as preachers, pastors, and theologians—creative, innovative, and undaunted by the remaining difficulties and barriers to their full participation as priests and bishops in the corporate life of the church. My own part has not involved regular parish commitments, but included celebrating the Eucharist and preaching, teaching, and giving spiritual direction, first at the General Theological Seminary and then more widely throughout the church, as well as giving workshops and retreats in seminaries, religious communities, and parishes.

My experience of this ministry differs somewhat from my experience as a laywoman, and the difference seems to me to be two-fold: I can preside at the Eucharist and pronounce absolution in the name of the Church, and I can and I must in all my public acts and words be mindful of the stewardship given me at ordination—the keys to the treasure of the church I am to use for unlocking those treasures for others. Ordination makes us public persons who can be called upon for service as housekeepers for the people of God.

When we are baptized into Christ, King, and Servant, we inherit the treasure. We acquire rights to it. It is embodied in various forms: "tradition," "apostolicity," "the faith," kerygma, sacrament. It lives at the heart of the church. All the ministries—ruling and obeying, suffering and healing, teaching and learning—must be done by all of us together, but no one person does them all. The varied ministries complete the whole. It is the special responsibility of the ordained ministry to keep the key of the treasure. This means both guarding the treasure against loss, inner contradiction, and decay, and making it available to all members of the Body.

I have come to see that the Good Shepherd is a pattern for the ministry of all Christians. It is an image that speaks of the total care of the flock and the total self-giving of the minister, even to death. It calls our attention specifically to the importance of knowing the flock by name, being known by them, and to the work of caring for them. This includes birthing, nourishing, gathering, healing them, and also helping them to die.

One day in 1979, when he was on a visit to the General Theological Seminary, I happened to meet Terry Holmes, then dean of the School of Theology at the University of the South in Sewanee, Tennessee. We had a little time to talk about spiritual direction and the teaching of spirituality. Later on that term I had a letter from him asking if I would go to Sewanee to work with him on the program in spirituality at the seminary there. I accepted the invitation, but leaving General Theological Seminary was a hard and painful parting. One of the seminarians took care of my luggage, and, as he was carrying the suitcases out to the taxi that was to take me to the airport, we encountered the dean, James Fenhagen, who was out walking his little dog. Jim said to me, "I hate to see this!" The taxi man opened the door, and the little square black hole looked to me like the entrance to a tomb. I got into it and was off to a new adventure at the age of seventy-one.

During my time at the seminary, I lived with the Sisters of St. Mary at their convent and retreat center, located a few miles out from the center of Sewanee on the edge of the Cumberland Plateau, looking west, with a beautiful view summer and winter. I shared in their life of prayer and to some extent in their community life. Sr. Lucy and I often took turns preaching and celebrating at the Sunday services in the convent chapel, always a happy occasion. Because the chapel was usually crowded, we opened the doors into the lobby where we put out extra chairs. After the service, breakfast was served to our many guests from the seminary and the surrounding area.

Ordination to the Priesthood

~

I have a lot to be thankful for—a lovely apartment, with enough space, a loving, accepting community where I both pursue my own interests and learning and have some personal interchange and common life, opportunities to celebrate the Eucharist and exercise a priestly ministry, teaching which I love, a good confessor. So I join you in giving thanks this Epiphany Eve for a deepened awareness of God's gifts to me through others.... (To Charlotte Moore, January 5, 1980)

~

I preached Saturday for the Sisters on their festival, the anniversary of the first professions and their patronal feast. I used the icon (the Baptism of Christ created by Joan Tuberty) and set the Purification in the perspective of the central mystery unfolded in the Epiphany season and symbolized in the Baptism. Then I invited my hearers to imagine another icon, yet unpainted, of Mary, overshadowed by the great wings of the Spirit, her feet down among the dark roots of the tree of Eden—spanning the whole of our experience, open to the dark instructive powers, to the Spirit, to everything between—the whole of ourselves called and sanctified by Him. (To Charlotte Moore, February 3, 1980)

~

Another joy from my Sewanee days was taking a "hermit day" every Saturday in a little hermitage fitted out with a kitchen, a fridge and a bed out at the end of the convent garden, overlooking the ravine. I used to spend the day there in prayer and silence.

~

A great deal is going on rapidly inside me and sometimes I'd like to stop the process and get off—but I can't. I could, you understand, in a way and I don't choose to. My Saturday retreats are important. I make them in different rhythms and styles, some structured, some not,

some restful and some challenging. (To Charlotte Moore,
June 23, 1980)

~

The sisters owned a good deal of land on top of that
mountain where I took many beautiful walks in the woods
filled with butterflies, one of my passions. During those
two years I saw more different kinds of butterflies than
during the whole rest of my life. The woods were also filled
with wild flowers of all kinds of colors—lavender, yellow,
pink—and were presided over by birds, every one of which
Sr. Kiara could name, identify, and tell its history. She
knew more about the birds than I did about butterflies,
even though I had a good bit of knowledge about them. I
did enjoy those walks enormously and those quiet days.
They were an oasis in my busy life.

While at the seminary I was not able to carry on a
"monastic breakfast" as I had at General, but I had a
prayer group one evening a week in the convent chapel.
Clifford Schane, the rector of the parish church and a
frequent visitor at the convent, asked me to give talks on
prayer at the church. I enjoyed my friendship with him in
both situations.

~

*Here is the sermon. It has too many undeveloped ideas in
it—like a stew with a banana peel and an orange rind
needing to be picked out....I just finished the 7 weeks
course on prayer at Otey Parish. It held up well and most
people were able to enter the silence and found the experience valuable....What a strange season we are in—
not yet Lent, the first daffodils are out! I made my
confession this p.m. Cliff is a real friend and we've
worked together a lot...On Ash Wednesday the entire
Seminary descends upon us for retreat. Moving of furniture, cleaning, as only nuns can and will clean—soup
and cheese for lunch. I think I will try for Lent to practice some of the simplicity recommended in Tilden Edwards'* Living Simply Through the Day: *being simply*

aware of what I'm doing, instead of racing my mind to solve problems and plan projects, for instance, at least some of them...I'm not convinced one should never work at problems or plans while making the bed or climbing the stairs.

Pilgrimage Home by Gerald May is a great help to me, with so much practical wisdom to help me, with so much practical wisdom about contemplative prayer formation for groups.... (To Charlotte Moore, March 1, 1981)

~

My work at Sewanee was to include team-teaching with Terry a course entitled "Introduction to Christian Spirituality," giving a course of my own on spiritual direction and, as a member of the adjunct faculty, taking my turn in celebrating the Eucharist, preaching, and any other activities related to being a faculty member.

Terry's introductory course in spirituality was required of all entering students. It met once a week and had regular assignments, a term paper, and an exam. Our chief text was Terry's *History of Christian Spirituality,* and we alternated between teaching and leading the follow-up discussion and prayer. During my first year of team-teaching with Terry, I learned something of his method and outlook. Working with him was a pleasure because he held up his end and supported me in my part. No matter how busy he was, he stayed through my presentations without interrupting except to ask questions in class discussions.

~

I am auditing Terry Holmes's course on mysticism and reading Bonaventure seriously for the first time. What struck me is the inner meaning of the vision of Francis at La Verna, of the crucified seraph—at the heart of darkness....The abyss (the luminous night of Gregory of Nyssa) is the cross, crucified love. Somehow this seems to put together the whole apophatic tradition of Pseudo-Dionysius, Gregory, John of the Cross, The Cloud of Un-

knowing—with the new theology of affect—from Bernard on.

(To Charlotte Moore, undated)

~

I set up the elective course on spiritual direction, designated as my sole responsibility, as a two-hour seminar meeting once a week. However, so many people wanted to take it that I had not only to divide the course into two sections but also offer it in both semesters. That kept me pretty busy. The customary pattern was for me to give a presentation in the first hour, then to devote the second hour to discussion and a case study by one of the students. The pattern for the case study was one I had learned at the Weston School of Theology in Cambridge, Massachusetts. After the student presented the case study, the group addressed the questions: What was being said, what was the response, how did we feel about it? The student presenter could join the discussion until it was time for the critique, but at that point the presenter was supposed to be silent until the end of the critique, when fifteen minutes was allotted for a response. The method was rather cut-and-dried, but I liked it and found it a good teaching tool.

~

Spiritual Direction: You are on the right track, I feel, in spite of the struggles. Every bit of new insight, (e.g., the need to apply your instinct for respecting other spiritualities, closer to home, etc.) is a treasure, but a costly treasure. Like you, I need to appropriate this new insight, and that is costly. (To Charlotte Moore, July 1, 1979)

~

The seminary gave me the use of an office in Bairnwick, a house on the outskirts of the campus, which was a very convenient, but rather noisy spot. I offered spiritual direction to students requesting it in the office there as well as at the convent.

~

Heard lots of confessions last night. It is one of the most humbling, and heart-breaking experiences of my ministry—this business of reconciliation—and what a wonderful, simple, life-giving sacrament, so homely, so concrete, so characteristic of the Lord who is really and truly, deeply and deliberately, to tally with us and for us and in our daily and weekly and yearly struggle! (To Charlotte Moore, March 6, 1981)

~

The uniqueness of each one is important, and monastic life has often failed to take this pole of our humanity into account. I'm glad that OSH has gone as far as it has to recognize and protect this uniqueness. But it isn't an ultimate, to which other things can be subordinated. I think of uniqueness and community or commonness as two poles, and in between are the types of schools or paths, rooted in a common Christian spirituality, but differentiated and yet grouped—and in tension both with the common source (tending to over- and underemphasize or neglect or unduly elevate aspects), and with the unique persons, who never entirely or permanently fit, and whose final rest will transcend them—in the energies of Love. (To Tilden Edwards, March 25, 1981)

~

Terry and I always spent at least an hour preparing for each of the class meetings. During those times we got into discussions on all kinds of subjects, especially when we talked about Jung, a special interest of Terry's. I am myself more skeptical than he was about some aspects of Jungian teaching and practice. It especially annoys me when Jung sets himself up as a biblical critic. Terry and I had many good arguments on this subject, but I never felt put down because I was a woman, for Terry always treated me as an equal.

Terry was a big man in body, mind, and spirit, and one had to get used to a big person's way of going at this work and handling himself. A man of such intellectual, moral, spiritual, and physical stature was bound to have a big impact on both the school and the university of which he was a part. His brain, his humor, his fearlessness, his loyalty, and his courtesy to his colleagues, including me, impressed me. Terry's wonderful sense of humor could get out of hand, sometimes on the bawdy side. He was, I think, used to an all-male group, but we were no longer that. There were a few women on the faculty and quite a number of women students. Sometimes his jokes at lunch upset us. He could hurt people, but he could also apologize. When most people would be circuitous, Terry was direct; that was good, for you knew where you stood. Sometimes I think he could even be a little of a bully. A couple of incidents illustrate this, one of them at my very first faculty meeting.

Normally I did not go to faculty meetings. I have no great taste for them, but this particular time I was especially invited to attend. Without warning, Terry put me on the spot: "Rachel, are you on the side of the faculty or the side of the students?" There I was, the confidante of so many people, both faculty and students. On various occasions I had listened to members of both groups and tried to respond according to my own sense of vocation, my own sense of my ministry, regardless of whether it was a faculty member or a student or someone else. I told Terry that in every institution I had ever lived in—and I had lived in a good many—there were always two sides to any issue. There was the administration and there was the rank and file. I considered myself to be open to both and not called to take sides in a controversy. Also, I tried to help each person who came to me to find the will of God in his or her own circumstances by asking the right question:

"What does God seem to be saying to you in all of this?"
My response seemed to satisfy the faculty, and the point
about whose side I was on was never brought up against
me again.

The question raised there—whose side was I on, faculty
or students?—has some relation to a question central to
life in a religious community. Something in me is rooted in
protest. It has to do with the way I listen to others, my
awareness of injustice and exploitation, selfishness, lust,
manipulation of others in the name of obedience. The incident at Sewanee evoked in me questions about obedience
itself because of my own experience, having myself had a
great deal of influence and authority in the religious life
from a young age.

As I reflect on experiences from the past, I think there
is also some connection between them and the position I
am in right now, when so many want to come and see me,
when to them time with me is precious. There is danger in
that too. Empathy can drain me. On the other hand, why
not? As my mother used to say, "What are you saving your-
self *for*?" What better thing have I to do with my very
limited energy? I think that I do understand more and
more clearly, however, in these last days, that I am a
channel, not a stream, not a spring, not even a well. And
the stream comes from the life-giving death of Jesus on
the cross, from that blood.

~

It seems as if for a lot of my life I've been torn between
being seen as a big, powerful, upright, influential person,
capable of helpfulness and insight and vision, but a little
scary—capable also of being an embodied conscience or
judge—'a lion on tiptoes—what is she up to now?'—and a
threat and a spoil-sport, to be left alone and guarded
against, even pushed out. I'm beginning to think I'm
some of all that, and that it doesn't matter very much.
I'm also a human woman....

I seem to do best when I leave that sort of reflection, let the negatives go—throw them up like paper in the wind, and react to demands, needs, opportunities, work, etc. as directly, simply, and honestly as I can, and 'the devil take the hindmost'—I mean by that, what am I saving my strength for? And whose strength is it anyway? (To Tilden Edwards, 19 August 1987)

~

To go back to the question before me at that faculty meeting, it was a question about loyalty. A student of mine once defined loyalty as "respect for that of which one is a part." My question has always been, "Can I listen to another in the context of the institution? In listening to others, what is my response, for instance, to accounts of suffering and humiliation caused by persons in authority, especially when I share in the authority of the institution by virtue of my position as a member of the faculty? Can I listen simply as a priest of the church and a spiritual friend, seeking only to help the speaker discern what God is saying through those particular circumstances? Can I refrain from judging or explaining or apologizing?

The other incident relating to Terry's tendency to bully was something he himself told me about after the fact. I had been invited to a dinner party at his house with six or eight members of the faculty. We had a very pleasant time; I enjoyed myself greatly, said thank you, and went home. In the next day or two he told me that he had deliberately invited some of the faculty members who had been opposed to my coming to the seminary in order to let them meet me and see whether they still thought they were right in their position. They had expected, I think, some black-clad, austere, humorless, negative kind of person who would be afraid to take part in discussing, eating, and drinking in the accustomed fashion of the faculty. Those present at the dinner party were disarmed by my taking part in a normal way. Although I was glad that Terry told me, it was a little disquieting all the same. I think perhaps that it was because I was not at first prepared for his unusual frankness about things.

While at Sewanee I also did some work with Terry on the text of a book he was writing, *The Spirituality of Ministry*, which turned out to be his last. I raised with him the issue of copy editing, the kind of editing that looks after split infinitives, spelling, and so on, because his own manuscripts tended to be very messy and badly spelled. They were dictated to a typist who knew neither Greek nor Latin, both of which he used freely without correcting anything. I started in to do the copy-editing, but he stopped me, saying, "Oh, no, that's up to the editors to do that, that's their job, they always do it." I think this is one reason why his book *The History of Christian Spirituality* is so flawed. It is full of errors, especially in the Greek and Latin, which could have been remedied by somebody like me. After Terry's death, when *Spirituality for Ministry* was being readied for publication, John Ratti, his editor, told me he wanted to make the book worthy of being Terry's last contribution. I raised the issue of copy-editing again. John Ratti said that yes, Terry was very inattentive to that part of his work and that on this score some of his books were not worthy of him. Because of John's desire to correct this situation in Terry's last book, he was grateful for my contribution as a copy editor.

My last talk with Terry before he left for what proved to be his last sabbatical took place in a big crowd where I had to crane my neck back to see his face way up there. He gave me some final, very loving words of encouragement and appreciation before leaving the whole department of spirituality, his course included, in my hands. It was of course a final farewell. He never returned from his sabbatical, for he died in the plane on his way home.

I went on with my teaching during Terry's sabbatical year.

~

I am beginning to gear up for the school year, have ac-
quired 2 reading courses besides my regular classes. One
is by Leo Rosenberg, an immense Jewish man with 5
years of rabbinical studies in Jerusalem—a recent con-
vert! Is he going to scare all of us to death? He knows a
lot. Terry has accepted him as a middler and wants him
to do the reading from the entire course for juniors with
me second semester. It should be interesting. (To
Charlotte Moore, September 7, 1980)

~

In teaching the introductory course on spirituality with
some help from David Killen and Tricia de Beer, I made
the mistake of using Terry's outline rather than devising
one of my own. Sometimes I got embattled and felt very
frustrated. One student wrote a very inadequate, flippant
reply to a test I gave. I flunked him. A few days later, I
was sitting on the ground, waiting for transportation,
when he came along and sat beside me. During our short
conversation I challenged him by saying, "You know perfectly well how to answer a question on a test. What made
you do that?" He replied, "Well, sometimes I can be stub-
born." To that I responded, "Yes, I know how that is!"
From that time on until the end of the term he was
cooperative.

~

Our seminar topic this week is on suffering and I'm
using, among other things, Jack McDuffie's little book,
Walk Out With Me. *Also Dorothee Soelle,* Suffering, *Til-*
den Edwards' *chapter in* Living Simply Through the Day
on "Aching," John of the Cross, Bk. 1 of Dark Night of
the Soul. *I would add: Origen, On Martyrdom and Gal-*
liwtzios' collection of letters from Nazi prison camps,
Dying We Live. *The literature is, of course, immense—*
there is Dante and Antigone and Oedipus Rex....I sup-
pose in spiritual direction the point is: how to stand with
those whose suffering cannot be taken away. The letters
from prison are heartbreaking but also strengthening.
There is such tender love expressed for those outside and

*such a spirit of serenity—most of the writers really
moved beyond bitterness and hatred. But what a sensi-
tive job it is to be with those we love in their suffering,
when we can't do anything else. So think of me with you,
remembering, praying, office after office, mass after
mass....* (To Charlotte Moore, November 1, 1980)

~

I was on the rota at the seminary for both preaching
and celebrating. One day when I assisted at the Eucharist
and it came time for the Holy Communion, I was distributing from one end of the rail and the Celebrant from the
other. I saw coming up the aisle a mother holding her
three year old child who was dying of an incurable birth
defect; she was a "blue baby" with a very short time to
live. As they came up the aisle on the opposite side from
where I was distributing Holy Communion, the little girl
pointed her finger at me and said to her mother, "I want it
from the lady." So I gave the little girl what was perhaps
her last Holy Communion.

Leaving Sewanee was a fresh trauma for me. I had already wept and bled over leaving Bolahun and then
General Seminary, and I wept and bled again in the same
way over leaving Sewanee after Terry Holmes died in
1981.

~

*I've decided that next year will be my last at the semi-
nary. I'm tired. I'm in my 70's. I need time unpressured
by deadlines and involvement in insoluble problems, to
learn to live differently, without drivenness about work,
listening to what I'm doing and feeling as well as to what
I'm thinking, and getting on with sorting out and drop-
ping off, with dying, that is. Also, if God gives me time,
doing some work on my papers, revising what I've already written.* (To Tilden Edwards, April 20, 1980)

~

This business of giving up is terribly hard for me, however convinced I am in my head. When I left Bolahun in 1965, I asked the drivers not to go through the school compound, but around through the hospital. I could not bear one more sight of the bafais and the teachers, the children I had worked with, loved for 5 years. And it tore my heart out to leave Margaret Hall School in 1959. Even leaving GTS was upsetting and very painful. Leaving Sewanee should be less of a wrench, but not easy. (To Tilden Edwards, November 2, 1980)

~

There are many people here I shall miss, with whom I've begun relationships—nourishing, delighting, growing. And my ministry here is very important to me....

I am trying to discern: what is God calling me to do next year on sabbatical: after leaving here? And trying to get some purchase on it by thinking over my sense of vocation to ministry, to ordained ministry, to monastic life. If I could feel I was part of something that was speaking, acting, being, for the servant church, I could put up better with the frustrations....

~

Transition seems to be a painful part of my own journey, and sometimes the bridges are tenuous indeed. How am I to go over, and where will this bridge lead me? As I thought about this, I recalled a leaving dream I had at Bolahun. I was with a group of sisters in an automobile, going along the road from the town by the elementary school compound to the fork where the road parted. One road went up to the girls' boarding compound, the other up to the convent. At the fork, the automobile continued with the rest of the sisters and left me alone at the fork. I walked along and was confronted with a river that was filled with snakes. Over it was a narrow bridge, hardly the width of my foot, and with no railings. Over the bridge were draped several snakes. I had in one hand a Bible and in the other hand a stick with which I could flick off the snakes and clear a path for myself.

I recall another icon of transition that also occurred in Bolahun. Sr. Marianne and I had been taken on a long walk through the woods to see a monkey bridge. A monkey bridge is a mysterious thing, said to be made by the native priests of the animist religion in that part of the world. How they do it no one seems to know. The bridges are high up by the river, from the tree on one side to the tree on the other, and are made mostly out of roots suspended from the tops of the trees. The way over is narrow, with a few planks to walk on and railings made out of the vines. When we drew near to the bridge, the boy who was leading us went ahead a little bit and then came back, his face shining. "Now I'm going to show you something wonderful!" Remembering this little vision helps me to face into the transition which is ahead of me now.

I returned to Vails Gate in 1981 to be reassigned to New York, to the house where I am now living, 134 East 28th Street, between Lexington and Third Avenues. Once more I had to enter a new group and tread easily, lightly, gently, until I could find my way, find my place in the community.

Travels in Jerusalem and Spain

O ne of the customs we at St. Helena's have copied from Roman Catholic communities of women is that a religious celebrating the fiftieth anniversary of her life vows may be allowed to make a pilgrimage to the Holy Land. So for my anniversary on July 26, 1986, I asked permission to do this and bulldozed Sr. Cristina into going with me. We were given permission and the wherewithal to make the trip. My friend Charlotte Moore flew with me to London a few days before Cris was able to leave her ministry in the South Bronx. Charlotte and I spent a few nights in a hotel there, getting over jet lag and exploring the neighborhood. Then we went to Fairacres in Oxford, Charlotte's first visit there. I was, as usual, given a seat in the choir, and Charlotte was allowed to visit with me all day long in a little parlor in the guest house. At night she went to the small nearby guest house of the All Saints Sisters.

It was my first visit to Fairacres after my ordination. At recreation that first afternoon, Mother Mary Clare came with her staff in her hand and sat at her usual place beside Mother Jane, who invited me to sit beside them. Mother Mary Clare looked quizzically at me and said, "Well, I suppose I should ask your blessing!" I said brazenly, "Yes, indeed, you should!"

For Charlotte, being in an enclosed convent was a new experience. She was especially diverted by being served hot water to drink at supper one night. I was quite used to that and did not find it strange. At the All Saints convent where Charlotte was staying, we met Bishop John V. Taylor and his wife, who were waiting for their quarters in Oxford to be ready for them. He had just retired. The first time I met him he was clutching a lovely purple shirt, which I think he had washed out himself and hung on the line to dry. He told me he cherished it because it was really purple, not cerise, and so it was.

The All Saints Sisters have a beautiful Ninian Comper chapel. They had begun a new ministry, that of maintaining a hospice for dying children, a place where parents and families can visit their children, but other visitors are not allowed. They also have a new and very flexible contemporary Rule replacing the old Victorian one. I enjoyed praying with them, having meals in their refectory, and seeing a little of them in the guest house.

Charlotte and I went back to London after our visit in Oxford, and from there Cristina and I took off for Tel Aviv by way of Amsterdam. In Amsterdam we had to change planes for Tel Aviv and experienced a process, soon to become very familiar to us, which included a very close scrutiny of every piece of our luggage and of our persons before being allowed to board the plane. We touched down in Tel Aviv in the evening. As dusk had already fallen, our first glimpse of the Holy City was simply of its walls and its silhouette. As we drove into the city, we went past bonfires which, we were told, had to do with a commemoration of the Maccabees by the Hasidim. We stayed at St. George's Cathedral hostel in a pleasant double room with plenty of space. We were able to go to daily office and the Eucharist at the Cathedral. One of the sisters of Grandchamp, Sr. Maatje from the small community at Ein Kerim, came to see us the next day and helped us plan our program.

We had decided we were not going on tours, because we were pilgrims, not tourists. We would make our own way by foot in the Old City, then hire a car and go first to the Dead Sea and then to Galilee. Walking about the Old City was our first real experience of Jerusalem. Maatje had advised us to begin by getting up very early and going up the Mount of Olives, so we bought one of those circular pieces of Arab bread, like soft bagels, and some coffee in a little shop, and then took a bus up to the Mount of Olives. From there we were to make the descent to Gethsemane and the Old City. We had our prayer books with us. When we looked out over the city for the first time from the Mount of Olives, I was struck by the sight of the Golden Gate. It was bricked up; I had not realized that. Clustering around it are graves of Muslims and Jews, all waiting for the coming of the Messiah. They want to be in the front seat when the Messiah comes; then the Golden Gate will be opened for the Messiah and all the elect. Ever since that day I have thought a lot about that beautiful bricked-up gate, pale yellow in the sun.

We made our way slowly down the narrow way leading to Gethsemane, stopping on the way at the chapel called *"Dominus Flevit,"* "the Lord wept." It is believed to be the place where Jesus looked out over Jerusalem and wept over it: "How often have I desired to gather your children together as a hen gathers her brood under her wings, and you not willing!" (Matt. 23:37) From there we went on to Gethsemane, where we stopped for prayer again in the garden and in the big basilica beside it.

Then we crossed over into the Holy City and entered, making the Stations of the Cross. We found our own way to do this, stopping sometimes in crowded shrines and at other times in rather lonely, empty places, until we reached the Church of the Holy Sepulchre where we prayed at the Anointing Slab and waited for our turn to approach the Shrine of the Holy Sepulchre itself. I was dismayed by the darkness and confusion, the rivalry of different Christian groups, the dust and the candle drippings. It seemed to me that everything that I wanted to see was covered up with dark, dusty velvet, gold braid and curtains. I could not really see anything much. I was told afterwards that this is often the first reaction of a pilgrim and that if you go back several times, you will come to a different mind. As it turned out, I was unable to get back, so I am afraid that is my only remaining impression of my visit to the Holy Sepulchre.

You are often told that on your first visit to the Holy Land you will have one great moment, and mine came at the Tomb of David. We had already visited the very beautiful Church of the Dormition and the Palace of Herod, where one sees those terrible dungeons and the place where Jesus' blood was shed at his scourging. Perhaps all that prepared the way for what was to come for me. As we left the church, we became aware of another building called the Tomb of David and decided to enter it. As I stepped over the threshold, I looked back through the door. In front of me was a scaffolding that partly blotted out some of the letters of those blue and white enamel signs which serve as street signs in Jerusalem. All I could see of the sign was *"Qol dami,"* which means "the voice of my blood." Whether there is such a sign or not I do not know—I suppose that I might have seen the second half of one word and the first half of another through the scaffolding. But as I turned around and looked into the Tomb of David, the words "the voice of my blood" echoed in my ears.

I approached a darkened stone ledge on which were set big candles with little markers under them. As I went close to one, I saw the word "Auschwitz." It overwhelmed me. I began to cry and sob, and I could not stop. We had a guide that day, something quite unusual for us. He withdrew quietly and tactfully and sat down to wait. I stood there weeping, sobbing, unable to do anything at all. Finally I said to Cris, "Please read to me from First

Corinthians 11." I wanted to hear something about blood that would help me bear remembering the blood of Auschwitz, Jesus' words about the Eucharist. And so she read aloud to me: "This cup is the new covenant in my blood. Do this, as often as you drink it, in remembrance of me." (v. 25) It quieted me enough so that we could go and kneel and pray together at the shrine called the Upper Room, the place of the Last Supper and the place of Pentecost, now a beautiful little chapel with red hangings. I had to go through with this experience of dread, of sorrow and grief, to feel it, to be overwhelmed by it.

As I was preparing to write this book, I looked back into the life of Rudolf Dreikurs, *The Courage To Be Imperfect*, by Terner and Pew, remembering vaguely that he had had some kind of experience in Jerusalem. I found that he, too, at exactly the same spot in the Tomb of David, before the candle marked Auschwitz, had been inundated with a sense of God. He found that he could pray. He had been an unbelieving Jew; his wife, a faithful Jew, often teased him about this business of not being able to believe.

As they landed in Tel Aviv for this their first visit to Jerusalem, she noticed that he was crying. She said, "What are you crying for? You're not a Jew!" (He used to say, "I'm a Jew by birth and a humanist by belief.") But in that moment at the Tomb of David, he was able to light a candle and to pray for his parents who had died at Auschwitz. It was a turning point for him as it was for me, and a strange coincidence. I seem still to meet him there.

After we had spent several days exploring the Old City on foot, Cris plunged into the job of hiring a car and came back triumphantly, with a little red Volkswagen. On our first venture in the Holy Land, with Sr. Maatje carrying a picnic lunch, we had driven through Jericho, down to the Dead Sea. We stopped first at the Mount of Temptation. Among other things I had wanted to climb a very high mountain during our time in the Holy Land. I did not know what I was asking for! Since I was not up to climbing any very high mountains, we decided that the Greek monastery on the side of the Mount of Temptation would be just about right. There were a few other pilgrims along the way. We spent some time in the chapel of the monks who lived there on the side of the mountain looking out over the hills in that strange desolate valley that leads down to the lowest place on the face of the earth, the Dead Sea.

Our next stop was Qumran. We had lunch there under a tree and then explored the ruins. It was quite startling to confront those great barren crags and wonder how on earth anybody got into a cave so high up and found the Dead Sea scrolls. But there they were. Now they are in the Museum in Jerusalem where later we saw them. From there we went to the Dead Sea itself, where Cris had a great swim. I stayed out; I did not feel like swimming, and besides we had only one bathing suit between us!

We also spent some time at Ein Kerim where the Sisters of Grandchamp have a small house on the site of the tomb of St. Elizabeth. The tomb is on the bottom level of the house; it is an open empty space which they have turned into a chapel and a shrine. Above are the sisters' quarters with their own chapel, where I had the privilege of celebrating the Eucharist for them. Down the mountain a little way is a Byzantine rite community of men whose monastery is dedicated to St. John the Baptist because it is built over his birthplace. We spent some time in their chapel praying with them.

We also visited Hadassah, the hospital nearby, to see the beautiful Chagall windows, and it was there that we met a young Jew, Yehezkel Landau, who is a leading member of an Israeli peace group called *Oz veShalom*. He is a strong, gentle, devout religious Jew, born in Hungary and educated at Harvard Divinity School. He is not a rabbi but a layman, and a very devout one, as well as being devoted to a nonviolent solution to his country's problems. He told us something of the way they went about their work.

Sometimes when Meir Kahane would go into an Arab village and terrorize the inhabitants, telling them they must get out or be killed, *Oz veShalom* would come in after them and give the opposite message. "We don't want you to leave. We want you to stay. We want you to be our brothers and sisters. We want to share the land with you. We are children of Abraham with you, and God has said that we are to take care of the stranger."

Another high point of our visit to Israel was a visit with Jill and Shim Leigh. Jill Holder and her older sister Valerie had been sent to the United States during World War II after their house in London had been bombed. They wound up at Margaret Hall School, since we were one of the few schools certified to take foreign students that could take both a fifth grader and an eighth grader. They were Jewish children, and we did our best to see to it that they had as good an education in their own faith as we were trying to give to the Christian girls. Consequently, when we got to Israel, we looked up Jill, who now lives near Lod.

She and her husband met us in Tel Aviv one afternoon and drove us to their house near a Children's Village. They took us first to see an old Orthodox church dedicated to St. George, a place of prayer and quiet with its ancient icons and burning lights. Later we went with them to see the graves of the Maccabees, great jagged stones upon a rocky outcropping overlooking the Jordan hills, and a castle built by the Mamelukes. Shim, Jill's husband, had lost a hand, I suppose in the war. Both are Israeli citizens; Jill works at the Children's Village, which is a school for both girls and boys with a very imaginative, creative program.

During our time in Jerusalem Cris and I made a visit to the Russian Orthodox Cathedral. We found the building locked and went to find someone at what looked to be the clergy house nearby. There we were invited in by a young priest who asked us to sit down on a bench in the hall while we stated our business. After giving us permission to see the cathedral, he disappeared, then returned shortly with a silent nun, dressed in a long black robe, a black veil with a sort of cap stamped with silver emblems on top it. She took us the whole way to the door of the cathedral in total silence, but her lips moved all the time. In our brief time in the place, we felt little sense of presence or radiance or life. The icons seemed to be modern prints. The nun then led us back in the same silence to the clergy house and disappeared into its depths. We said goodbye to the priest, having experienced a strange interlude without resonance, without any sense of reality. We returned thankfully to St. George's.

The last thing we did before getting ready to leave for home was to take a trip by car to Galilee. We drove up along the Jordan to Tiberias, then along the Lake of Galilee to a place called Tabgha where there is a beautiful Benedictine monastery. The church there is built over the remains of a famous fourth century mosaic pavement commemorating the miracle of the loaves and fishes. We spent a night or two in the small guest house there. When it came time for the Eucharist, we were invited to join the monks and their guests. As we stood around the altar in the small side chapel—about ten of us—we were asked not what church we belonged to, but what language we spoke. The celebrant wove all those languages into the Eucharist—English (which he did not know much of), German, French, a little Hebrew, a little Latin. Also on the shore of the lake was a place reserved for silent prayer; it had a stone altar, a very simple boulder surmounted by a cross and protected by a kind of thatched roof. It was a wonderful place to go early in the morning; we said Matins there as we looked out over the Sea of Galilee. It was there at the Sea of Galilee that Jesus seemed very close, much more so than in the Church of the Holy Sepulchre or any other shrine that we had seen.

I hated to leave, but time was limited. We packed a
lunch and set out westward for the coast, for our last stop
which was at Caesarea. We drove to Nazareth too late in
the day to enter the church there. The whole city was disappointing, confusing; we were glad to get out of it. Going
into the ruined fortification of Caesarea was a different experience. I was appalled by the layer upon layer of de-
struction, century after century, everything Jewish
destroyed by the Romans, everything Roman destroyed by
the next lot, and then the next lot, layer upon layer of
broken, smashed, ruined holy things. After we went
through the great gateway—all that remains of the
Crusader fortifications—we had some lunch in one of the
little restaurants within and then took a swim in the blue-
green Mediterranean, taking turns with our one bathing
suit. After that we had a chance to drive through a kibbutz
on the way back to Tel Aviv and Jerusalem, where we
started to pack for going home.

On our last full day we decided to go to Bethlehem,
something we had not yet done. It proved to be
catastrophic. We went through the Old Basilica, airless,
crowded, and to me irrelevant, and came out into the
newer Franciscan church. As I was standing in the entrance, suddenly I was shoved from behind. A strong arm
pushed me smack down on my back and I knew when I fell
that I had broken my back—I know what it feels like.
People crowded around me. I begged them not to sit me
up. Someone called an ambulance. One of the men around
was a doctor whom I asked to please stay with me until I
was on a stretcher and into the ambulance so that others
would not injure me more.

The man who did it, I learned afterwards, was half-
blind and rather feeble-minded and was employed by the
Franciscans as a porter. Apparently he had heard a bell
somewhere and came thrashing up in his lumbering way
to answer it. He came from behind me; I never saw him.
He shoved aside whatever was in his way, including me.

Cris and I rode by jerks through the streets of Bethlehem and back to Jerusalem, first to a hospital on Mount Scopus where they refused to accept me because they had no orthopedic ward. Then, taken from stretcher to stretcher, shouting all the time, "O God, O God!", I finally wound up at Hadassah Hospital. There I waited in the Emergency Room with no treatment, nothing for pain, until two in the morning when I finally landed in a bed. They never did give me anything for pain except Tylenol. It was quite an experience; I was there for eight days in a cast made on an elastic base so that it could open down the front. While I was flat on my face in the plaster room, a soldier came in demanding to have his cast taken off by the technician, right then and there. They argued a bit, and finally the plaster man left me and took his drill; zip, zip, zip, wham! went the plaster cast and off went the soldier. Back came this very skillful, gentle man to finish me up. Because Hadassah is a military hospital, soldiers have first claim. Another time when Cris had gone off to do something, I was suddenly told that there was military drill or alert and that my calls for pain medication (Tylenol) could not be answered. Nor were they ever answered! I did not know what had happened to Cris until the next morning when I discovered she had been shoved out the door for the air raid drill.

Much of the treatment I received was very good. Their technicians, their social workers, the male nurses, especially the Arab ones, were skillful and courteous. The women tended to be noisy, clattered about on wooden clogs, and were not as good at their job as the men. The food was monotonous, for it consisted of the soft yogurt and raw vegetables of the Israeli diet. On Sabbath nothing was done, and leftover food was served. A nurse came and poured water over my hands; that was all the bathing I got from her until Saturday at sundown. Everything stopped. Fortunately, I had Cristina with me to bring me real coffee every morning and give me a bath when I needed it. Also, the sisters from Ein Kerim came and sat with me. One day Soeur Jacoba came to see me with her sewing stashed away in her hat. She spent the morning with me, so gently, so lovingly, while she worked on the sewing. We had such a pleasant time together! She had met me before when she was in New York and I had taken her to the United Nations building where we saw the Chagall window and the great pendulum, which she remembered especially.

The journey home was also memorable. Cris spent the night before in the hospital on a couple of chairs beside me in bed. We had to get up very early and get into a private ambulance, which took us to the airport. There Cris left me in a wheelchair while she went off to deal with the luggage. As she turned around and saw me, she came back and said to me, "Rachel, don't look so alert!" She was afraid somebody would think I was a fake!

Eventually we landed at JFK in New York, where Sr. Andrea and Sr. Cornelia waited for us in great frustration. The ambulance they had ordered from a private outfit had its orders wrong; consequently, there was no ambulance. By chance, a couple of young women came rocketing up in a small ambulance, depositing somebody, and they agreed to take me to Roosevelt Hospital. It was a wild ride. For some reason I thought of them as the "Purple Rose of Cairo," a movie I had seen before I left the United States. They were young, they chattered about their dates, they did not know the way, and we got lost a number of times. Finally we reached Roosevelt Hospital at 7:30, having left JFK at 5:00. And that was the end of my jubilee pilgrimage.

I will never forget some of the experiences there, but the strange experience at the Tomb of David was the high and low point of the pilgrimage for me. It was in a sense the meaning of my broken back. It had to do with my cry of pain, "O God, O God," as I was taken through those streets in the ambulance and passed from pillar to post, and waited, waited, waited in that pain. Linking it up with the experience of Dr. Dreikurs deepens my sense of awe about it. Perhaps I shall understand more of it some day. "The voice of my blood," words of dread and words of power, and the overwhelming rush of tears and wrenching sobs there in that place where Auschwitz is remembered.

I spent some time at Vails Gate convalescing from my accident. At the beginning of the Long Retreat, the community celebrated the Golden Anniversary of my life profession with a feast served out of doors, as well as skits and songs and speeches. It was a pleasant time. It was hard for me to take in that I had been under life vows for fifty years, but that is the fact.

In September I took up my work again at General Theological Seminary, where I was an adjunct professor, and started again with two prayer groups, one in the evening and the other a "monastic breakfast" the next morning. The Dean gave me a small apartment, which he dedicated as Julian House in a service one evening and set apart to be used only for prayer and spiritual direction. It is a pleasant little place with a sitting room in the front that has a stove and a fridge so that I can prepare some refreshments for my prayer group and the monastic breakfast. A corridor leads back to a little bath and a bedroom that gives onto Twentieth Street, a very comfortable place, small and unpretentious, but well suited to my needs. I spent Wednesdays and Thursdays there and overnight so that I could have the evening and early morning prayer groups.

~

The work of Julian House is growing—a big prayer group, two "monastic breakfasts" each week, lots of directees...

The pressure of outside calls for support for causes close to my heart—S. Africa, Peace, puts more pressure as I struggle to sandwich things in and leave us time for doing my laundry and mending my clothes or getting some rest. But I figure: if God gives me all this energy, what am I saving it for? Use it while I have it. (To Tilden Edwards, October 25, 1985)

~

I've been doing a lot—regular direction at GTS, two prayer groups, a reflection group, three justice and peace workshops at a parish...

The sense of urgency about our future course as a nation is what impels me. If I die of it (which I don't expect, of course), how better to die? (To Tilden Edwards, November 4, 1986)

~

By this time *Gender and God,* my first book undertaken on my own, had been published, freeing me to spend more time doing spiritual direction. This book, named in my own mind as *F/M: Image of God,* was a long, hard job, and many people gave me great help in its completion. My community was very willing to free me from all other responsibilities every morning until noon. Others helped me with individual chapters and Fontaine Belford with overall problems. Cynthia Shattuck at Cowley Publications was responsible for the final editing and the book's present form.

During this same period, I was asked to join the diocesan Peace Task Force and did some workshops and preaching for them. After my return to New York, I had also been going as a regular parishioner to St. Luke-in-the-Fields. One Sunday I took the bus as usual down to the crosstown bus on Eleventh Street, and as I was walking across Third Avenue towards the bus stop, I saw a man standing there with his hat over his eyes, his face half-muffled. I said to myself, "He is not waiting for a bus." However, I walked by him nonchalantly, holding my purse by its strap (which one should never do in New York City) and the next thing I knew he had come behind me and given me an expert shove between the shoulders. I saw my arm go up like a windmill, pocketbook at the top; then I saw my pocketbook disappear, and I landed flat on my face. My glasses flew off, and I just barely missed hitting the iron balustrade beside some steps leading down to an apartment house entrance. As I tried to dust myself off and get up, I was surrounded by women who came up from the tenements and sat down on either side of me, wiped off the blood, thrust into my hands some money in change, brought ice to put on my face, called the police and the convent. As I sat there, I thought, "How am I going to get to church?"

Police came with their ambulance van, tested me, and asked me if I would please be willing to go to the nearest hospital and be checked over. Meanwhile, Sr. Cintra had arrived, and a young man on a bicycle had taken off after the thief. As we sped along to St. Vincent's in the back of a police car, I heard them announce to headquarters, "Proceding to St. Vincent's Hospital with two female nuns in the back seat!" The two female nuns were checked into the Emergency Room; I was examined and pronounced sound. I had scrapes and was in a certain amount of shock, but nothing was broken. For a time I continued to go to St. Luke's, where I was a member of the Peacemakers Group, but eventually I realized that it was not really a good use of my energy to get myself crosstown and downtown on Sunday when the city is so deserted. I transferred to nearby Calvary Church, where my first work in the city had begun, and am still happily a member there.

During the summer of 1987 Sr. Madeleine's community, the Sisters of St. Mary in Sewanee, gave her a month's holiday and suggested that she visit Grandchamp and then go to Spain. They asked me if I would go with her. Madeleine had completed her time in office as Sister Superior, and this was a short sabbatical for her. She came east and went about getting a French visa, a difficult business because of very long lines. Since we would have to go through France on our way from Geneva to Barcelona by train, both of us needed French visas.

We flew to Geneva and from there went by train to Neuchatel, spending two weeks at the community of Grandchamp. I was in my old room *"Louange"* ("Praise") in Amandier, which I have always loved. It seemed to welcome me. I found the sisters newly interested in feminism, especially the young ones, and the second weekend we were there a group of German feminists came for a weekend and their annual meeting. So it was quite in keeping that they asked me to celebrate the Eucharist and to preach on the Feast of the Holy Trinity.

I took my text from Julian of Norwich and spoke about her doctrine of the Trinity, and then celebrated half in French and half in English. I like especially the Taizé rite, with its Invitation to Holy Communion—*"Venez, car tout est prêt."* "Come, for all is ready." The young sisters were reading Rosemary Radford Reuther, Elisabeth Schüssler Fiorenza, Phyllis Trible, Elisabeth Wendel-Moltmann, and many other feminist writers of our day. They were very interested in working out a liturgy that would express the wholeness of the Christian people and the wholeness of our experience.

While at Grandchamp, Sr. Madeleine and I were assigned to a *foyer*, she in one, I in another. Sharing again in *révision de vie* was, as always, a comforting and enlightening experience. One Saturday the two *foyers* were combined, and together we rode up to the Jura Mountains to a small chalet one of their friends was giving the community, carrying with us the makings of tea, bread and chocolate. And there, high up on the top of the mountain, we spent some time reflecting together on the meaning of the Holy Trinity. We looked out over pasture lands, flocks, outcroppings of rock, brilliant Alpine flowers, including gentians with their beautiful deep indigo blue. Afterwards, Soeur Madeleine of Grandchamp drove us home through the lovely, peaceful countryside.

In Spain we began with a few days in Barcelona, then hired a car and drove to Zaragoza, to Burgos, to Salamanca, stopped at Santo Domingo de Silos, then to Avila, Toledo and Madrid. My best and most joyous memories of Barcelona center on the Picasso Museum, the Romanesque galleries in the great museum overlooking the city, and the strange, fascinating works of Gaudi, the architect. These looked to me like sand castles I used to make when I was a little girl, dripping water and sand to make little towers and minarets. I remember also a little restaurant around the corner from our hotel where you could get a *paella*, and the waiter's face one evening when Sr. Madeleine got her calculations wrong by one decimal point and overpaid him ten times! He corrected her and handed back the money, clucking his disapproval. I remember walking up and down Las Ramblas, a wide street lined on each side with flower stalls, bird cages, food hawkers, tricksters of every kind, newspaper kiosks—a street haunted, we were told, by pickpockets.

The most memorable cathedral was, for me, the one in Burgos, a city that also celebrates Franco with an equestrian statue and a boulevard named for him. In Zaragoza we were struck by the way the cathedral and the Templo del Pilar were placed side by side; the cathedral, shabby but beautiful in its Romanesque simplicity, degraded to the status of a parish church, and the newer Templo del Pilar, which is larger, more ornate, heavier, with its great screen dividing the choir from the laity. When we tried attending Mass in the main church of the Templo, both the architecture and the preacher, who seemed to be giving an angry diatribe, drove us out. We took refuge in a small side chapel which had a curious ivory figure of Christ in a skirt, green for feria and red or white on feast days. The statue was very old, and traditionally attributed to Nicodemus himself. As we entered, Mass was already in process; we could follow the movement but not the words.

In spite of this, there was something welcoming about that group; we felt ourselves at home from the beginning. Madeleine whispered to me, "Not Spanish." I knew it was not Latin; we both knew it was not French or German, yet the congregation made its responses. At the Peace, we were really greeted. When the priest realized that he had only one host and no key to the tabernacle, he sent the layman who was serving him for the key and invited the congregation to keep on singing. The man returned empty-handed. Another emissary was sent; he also returned without the key. The priest was very relaxed, quite undisturbed by all of this. Presently a little potentate whose band proclaimed him to be the cathedral sacristan came down the aisle with the key which he solemnly, and not too willingly, relinquished to the priest. We felt it right that day to receive Holy Communion, the first time in Spain that we had done so. Later, in one of the side chapels, we ran into some of the people and discovered that the group was of Hungarian descent and on a pilgrimage from Canada. The language of the Mass was Hungarian; our mystery was solved.

A visit to *Huelgas Reales* (Royal Retreat) outside Burgos, a place where the royal family could go for their devotions and be entertained by enclosed Dominican nuns, proved to be another highlight for us. In the museum there were portraits of the reigning abbesses, complete with croziers and facial expressions of dominance, not to say arrogance. I would not want to ask a permission from one of them! Also outside Burgos we visited a lovely Romanesque monastery, Santo Domingo de Silos, where we were met for the first and only time in Spain by the resident monks. Nowhere else did we see hide or hair of the religious who owned the great museums and cloisters. After welcoming us, the Santo Domingo monks sent us off on a tour led by seminarians. The cloister was exquisite, as was the museum, but most heartwarming of all, however, was the sight of one of the monks with a baby he had just baptized, for the monastery is also a parish church.

In Salamanca in the cloister of the Dominican nuns there, I discovered the tomb of an African woman. I knew that the name must be African. At the little booth where cards were sold and entrance fees collected, I picked up a pamphlet and just as I had thought, it told the story of a seventeenth-century African woman who was captured from what is now Ghana and taken to Spain, where she lived in a noble family who was kind to her. She had already been converted to Roman Catholicism and was finally allowed to try her vocation with the enclosed Dominican nuns there. Triumphantly I took the little pamphlet home to give to our Ghanaian sister, Rosina.

Salamanca also has the ancient university where Teresa of Avila came to make her confession to one of the Dominican friars and where Luis de León taught until his imprisonment for heresy—he translated the Song of Songs into Spanish and preached about it! The very classroom in which he taught, with its little pulpit and its log benches, has been kept intact. From that pulpit Luis de León, back after years of imprisonment for his heresy, took up his teaching again. The story goes that he mounted the pulpit, calmly surveyed his audience, and began: "As we were saying...."

Much of the pleasure of our journey was simply driving through the countryside, watching the mountains to the north as we went from Barcelona to Burgos, and then turning south through mountains, by deep green lakes, great fields of pale golden grain with red poppies, and stopping by the wayside for a picnic lunch. We noticed how few places were really wooded; everything seemed to be cultivated or else barren.

In Avila it seemed as though we met Teresa and John of the Cross in person; their joyous spirit, their simple everyday presences were preserved in the museum at the Convent of the Incarnation. Teresa's musical instruments, her little kitchen, samples of her handwriting, and the chair in which John of the Cross heard confessions are all there. The noticeable lessening of ornamentation and crowning with flowers there than in many other places helped us to feel much closer to those two great spirits.

Toledo holds interesting memories of the Spanish Jews in their Sephardic synagogue. The lovely museum of the Holy Cross, not on the tourist list, was not crowded. From its ceiling hang the battle flags of Lepanto, and its fine collection includes paintings, sculptures, and many artifacts. James Michener in his book *Iberia* writes,

> Walking one night along the ramparts of Avila, I reasoned, "If Spain had kept her Moors, her agriculture and manufacturing would have prospered. If she had kept her Jews, her commercial management would have kept pace with England's. If she had retained a few inquiring Protestant professors, her universities might have remained vital, and if she had held on to her *illuminati*, her spiritual life would have been renewed...but she wouldn't be Spain."

I have thought a great deal about this comment by Michener, and it seems to me to be profoundly true. I found Spain a tragic place for the very reason that she had not been able to deal with her opposites and had instead banished and destroyed them and their works—the Moors, the Jews, the Protestants, and the *Illuminati*. It was tragic because she refused to deal with opposition; she had a tendency to silence those who disagreed, unable to tolerate ambiguity and uncertainty.

After Toledo we headed for Madrid, where we had quite a time finding the Reformed Anglican Church where we intended to stay. Under Franco a Protestant church had not been allowed any distinguishing marks on its facade; consequently, the cathedral is flush with other buildings on a side street. When we finally did find it, going inside was like coming home. The dean and the bishop and his wife received us with great warmth, gave us rooms in their guest quarters, and allowed us to share in their worship. This church has close links with the church in Ireland; that means it is very low church and its liturgy is influenced by the Irish church. It uses the Mozarabic rite for the Eucharist, a new experience for us.

On our journey in Spain we saw mostly cathedrals, cloisters, museums, and a great deal of fine medieval and Baroque architecture. The emphasis was on miracles, bloody martyrdoms, flower-crowned virgins and saints, and the separation of the laity from the sanctuary by ornate screens. Museums tended to be airless and crowded, especially the El Greco Museum in Toledo and the Prado in Madrid. As I reflected on my experiences there, I decided that a person from Mars taking the same journey would believe that Jesus was born of a virgin, was crucified and died a horrible, bloody death, and then crowned his mother in heaven, period! There are very few representations of Jesus as a teacher, as a healer, as a preacher, and very few images of the Resurrection, perhaps partly because these are not as easy to represent in stone or in color as nativities and crucifixions and crownings in heaven. Not until we got to the Prado and saw the El Greco did I see a resurrection or a picture of Mary as a real human being, a peasant woman. What a joy that was!

As I waited for Matins to begin this morning, sitting down here in the guest floor of the Manhattan convent, I thought about my little cell "Louange" at Grandchamp. I began to ask God how I can offer my praise in the midst of this dying life of mine. I am healing and dying at the same time. I am aware of the natural power of healing within my body, giving me more strength and a little more endurance each day, a little more clarity of mind, a little more focus, a little more ability to plan and to hope. At the same time I am also aware of the growth of my disease, the development of new lumps, cancerous lumps, in my belly. Both strains, health and bodily dying, are woven together. They uphold me in a strange way because they are both *there* and *real* in this world that God has made. I ask God to teach me how to use my tongue, my mind, my heart, my praise to speak out of this double consciousness, this interwoven sense—praise from the depths, praise for life, praise for death, praise for community, for solitude and for the earth.

I began to think about T. S. Eliot's *Four Quartets*, the line about the broken king returning to Little Gidding, "where prayer is valid," and of the contrast between that and the Little Gidding of Eliot's day. It was not much more than a few ruins, and yet it was still for him a place where prayer was valid. And I think, "Where is prayer valid?" I think about Grandchamp, about that little cell, about my experience there of prayer, about the big chapel, L'Arche, about the poustinia, about times by the river, by the lake, up in the Juras, and about this dying life of mine where prayer is also valid.

My praise must come from my healing and ruining body, out of that two-fold experience of returning life and going down in defeat, into death and nothingness to the unknown, the unknowable, into the abyss of God. The two threads of my life now are dread and praise, woven together in my daily life, saying goodbye, hoping for respite. This seems to be my approach to God each day and each night. In dying we live.

Looking Back

As I think back over my life and look for the experiences out of which I have grown and changed, a number of episodes come to mind. In reflecting on how I have moved from my early conversion experience at St. John the Evangelist Church on Bowdoin Street in Boston, where I was fed a straight Anglo-Catholic line that I embraced happily and completely, I realize that I act not merely on feelings nor from my head alone, but have always tried to join the two. When I am moved by compassion, for instance, I do not act until I have really thought about it and seen some glimmer of a way through, but I do not try to analyze it and figure it out to the last dot. Once I can see that glimmer, I tend to go ahead. I cannot remember a time when I believe that this has played me false. I do not act simply on feelings, for my own feelings are far too unreliable for that. We all need to bring both feelings and intellect into focus in some way. I suppose that in different personalities the mix, the preponderance of one over the other, is different. Perhaps if both these elements were entirely equal, we would never do anything. The way I work toward a conclusion out of my general sense of what is right, rather than a precise theological analysis, is shown in the way I came to think about intercommunion.

Gradually I felt more and more deeply that the Eucharist is God's feast, God's table, and that we have no right to keep one another from sharing in that table. Anyone who believes in Jesus Christ and wants to receive that Body and Blood, any Christian, should be able to approach the Holy Table. The same thing would hold true for anyone who, although not ordained, believed him or herself to be called to celebrate the Eucharist. During the late 60s, at a conference in Belgium, I had to decide what to do about a mass celebrated by one of the brothers at Taizé. Would I receive, or not? I had no doubt whatever that the Taizé Eucharist was valid. When the celebrant turned to the congregation and said, *"Venez, car tout est pret,"* "Come, for all is ready," I could not stay away.

I also remember a deaf friend of mine, a minister of the United Church of Christ, who used to visit us in Kentucky. During the Eucharist he would remain kneeling at the back of our small convent chapel while the rest of us went forward to receive the Blessed Sacrament. I felt awful about that. Consequently, it was a great joy for me subsequently to be able to jump over that barrier. When I was in my first year of divinity studies in Toronto, I was invited to the graduation exercises of Emmanuel College of the United Church of Christ. I went to my own dean and asked him if he thought I would be "letting down the side" if I received at Emmanuel. He very lovingly and gently told me to do whatever my conscience bade me do; as a result, I took part in a Protestant eucharist for the first time. It was certainly a great joy to me when our own church passed a resolution opening Holy Communion to baptized members of other Christian churches.

My whole community has now moved from its early Anglo-Catholic ritual, theology, and spirituality into a far more open stance. More than anyone else, it was Frank Gavin who first opened the way for us through his addresses at the 1933 Blue Grass Conference on the prophets and the creed. He was still a whole-hearted Anglo-Catholic—"High as the sky!" he used to say—"The sky's the limit," but he believed in using one's head. Once he told me, "You must follow the truth no matter where it leads you, even if it leads you out of the church." For me, Fr. Frank's attitude was life-saving because it meant I have been able to listen to my doubts and follow them.

Early in my life as a religious, during my year at Arlington Heights, I set aside one hour every week to consider my doubts and difficulties. I called it "Office Hours for Jitters"! When I felt jittery about the faith or troubled about something in my environment, I would say, "I'm busy now. Come back on Saturday morning at 10 and you can have all the time you want." During that hour I would write down my dialogues with doubts and jitters on yellow paper.

Around that time, Fr. Frank also recommended to me a book by W. G. Peck, *The Social Implication of the Oxford Movement,* along with some books on what was then called "the new psychology." These books opened us out in two directions, one towards social action, so that we had to discover the relationship between the High Church rituals we were so keen on and questions of war and peace, anti-Semitism, and racism. Segregation was certainly part of our lives in Kentucky at that time, and it was against the law for us to take a Black student at Margaret Hall School. But very early on I made contact with a Black school in Versailles and saw to it that our senior class visited it. Our students needed to see and to experience the difference between what they had in an all-white school and what the Black students had. After spending some time visiting the Black school, our girls talked about the differences and recognized clearly that the two schools were not at all "separate but equal."

The "new psychology" began to open us out to the realities that had been stuffed down into the unconscious by the negative spirituality inculcated by our own rule and that of many other religious orders as well. Books on repentance and confession tended to reinforce the idea that feelings of anger, resentment and envy are wicked and need to be confessed and rooted out. I believed all these teachings and strove to root out all these feelings. It was a long time before I came to terms with the fact that my feelings, my passions, are given by God, and it is up to me to recognize, welcome, and use those feelings effectively, not deny or resent them. I needed to refrain from injuring others with my anger and my resentment and to recognize my jealousy of other people, how envious and lustful I was, without forcing myself to repent. Repentance meant, in those days, that you were not going to do it any more. And how can you say that you are never going to be lustful or envious or jealous or angry anymore, when those passions are all part of our human nature?

It took me a long time to accomplish this gradual shift in consciousness and in ethical, moral and spiritual responses to life. Going to confession was a horror. I made the mistake of reading more and more moral theology which presented these questions from the viewpoint of scholastic theology. All this simply reinforced my fears. At the same time I was reading more in the field of psychotherapy, primarily Freud, even though my confessor warned me against him. Since I always tried to read both sides of an issue, I also read St. John of the Cross and Teresa at the same time as Freud; to me this seemed a very good combination. But my confessor said, "I think you've had enough of that." I think he was wrong; to look at both sides is something I have always needed and still continue to need.

During my first talk with him, Fr. Frank also urged me to read the famous collection of essays called *Lux Mundi,* which marked the first time Anglican theologians tried to come to grips with modernity late in the nineteenth century. I remember sitting on the floor of my cell reading away on the essay on faith and finding it very liberating. After that I went on to *Essays Catholic and Critical,* which took me a little further in my thinking. All during this time I was also reading Thomas Aquinas, going all the way through the *Summa Theologica* in English, every one of those dark red volumes from beginning to end. The works of Maritain and Garrigon-LaGrange gave me much pleasure, but in time I began to get enough of them. My own writings of that period reveal that I was imbued with that whole scholastic theological system, which later was to be dismembered piece by piece, with great pain and anxiety, without anything to put in its place.

Liberation theology and creation theology are very helpful to me, but I would not say that either one is *my* theology. Liberation theology, in my opinion, can be very one-sided; I think creation theology is in need of more work, which it will no doubt receive over time. The theology of Moltmann has been very important to me, especially his last volume on creation, but somehow it has not yet reached as full a development as I believe it will. Feminist theology also seems very one-sided to me, but at the same time absolutely necessary. It has to develop on its own, I believe, but I have to integrate all these insights into my own theology and spirituality, a task I do not expect to complete.

My own method begins with Scripture. Whenever I preach, what I say is rooted in that week's passages from Scripture, which I read carefully with the best exegetical skills I know. In working with the texts, I am open to what other commentators have said, to my own experience and insights, and open, I hope, to the people who are going to listen to what I have to say. I read the Bible out of a deep love for the tradition. I can love the Greek Fathers and Augustine—and I do love them—without embracing their negative spirituality. I can see their love, their devotion to the faith; I can see where they come from; I am very grateful for all they have taught me, but I am not a traditionalist.

When I was writing my thesis for the S.T.M. at General Seminary, I told my advisor, Dick Norris, "I'm a Bible nut." When he said, "You'll have to get over that!" I answered, "No, I don't think that I ever will." We had many a tiff over many subjects, including that one! I wanted to write about poverty, and he wanted me to write about chastity. I won! Working on the topic of poverty under his direction was a most useful exercise, for it gave me a whole year to immerse myself in the church fathers and resulted in a lasting love for them despite my awareness of the limitations of patristic theology. I cannot be a theological fundamentalist; this leaves me a little vague sometimes but not unanchored, for I am anchored in the Bible. I believe that the Holy Spirit brought forth the tradition, but I do not believe that the tradition is infallible any more than the Bible is. The Bible has some ugly spots which I have to probe deeply in an effort to discern what the Spirit is trying to tell me, but it has never stopped being the deepest source of my spiritual nourishment.

One of the weaknesses of people like me is that, although we depend upon a central vision—a common faith and obedience—for our own inner strength, we tend to neglect the contributions of a common faith and obedience to that central vision. Little by little we begin to confuse it with our own particular visions, plans, and convictions. Of course, leadership and creative ideas, along with their development and practical implementation, are of primary importance, but we may have a weak grasp of both the cost and the pay of focusing them and bringing them to fruition. I remember a young novice saying to me, "When you put something in, you want to see something come out on the other end."

Writing this book, piece by small piece, in the bed or propped up in a chair beside it, has impressed me so much in general with the relationship between vision and drudging—typing it up, getting it going, tidying, directing, and developing. I see the importance of finding the right way to express and carry out the common vision of justice and peace—covenant peace—which was given us by the Holy Spirit, bit by bit, in our darkness and error as well as in our moments of real insight.

My thoughts about independent secondary schools, at
least the few I still know about in my own country, seem to
incorporate many of the ideas and ideals that were important to me over the years: fields of study related to each
other or to wider and wider issues and visions and service
to the community, now emphasized in many independent
secondary schools. There seems to be a movement towards
a more holistic overview of education. At the same time,
there is a clamor for the teaching of values that are much
deeper, more significant, and of higher priority for both individuals and collectives than considerations of purely
personal gifts and needs. I hope the time will come when
the independent schools will recognize their common calling and put all the riches they have at their disposal into
working together for this common goal, for our country, for
the world and for God's creation in the universe.

As for seminary education, I would advocate a push
towards this same commonality so that schools of theology
everywhere would work more and more closely with each
other. At the same time, out of this commonality worship,
study, community activities and all of the separate courses
within each school would grow towards wholeness within
and outreach to others, however different, in search of the
shalom of God common to us all. I would like to see interior rifts healed—rifts between "hard" and "soft" subjects
and their professors, between the tenured and untenured.
For example, I would like to see every venture, every new
idea clearly defined in relation to the common good of seminaries. A common worship related both to the common
pursuit of truth in theological study and to the deep interior moving of the Spirit, that meeting of our God with our
desires and needs, should be the life-giving force to all our
work as teachers and administrators in our seminaries.

As for religious life, that is in some ways the hardest
question of all for me. I hope for a sense of urgency in our
response to the call of God to a "dedicated life," the life of
the traditional threefold vow of poverty, chastity and obe-

dience. I hope this basic call will bring us together, men and women, Catholic and Orthodox and Protestant, Anglicans among themselves, and open us up more and more towards the recognition of the meaning of our common vision *for the world.*

The months following my return from Spain during the summer of 1987 were filled with various activities—responsibility for writing reviews, preparing workshops and giving them, but mostly three or four full days every week in giving spiritual direction at General Theological Seminary. I remember puzzling times of illness, weariness, strange fleeting symptoms without stable diagnosis, until at last cancerous tumors were spotted, diagnosed, and surgically removed. Since then I have had to face increasingly the knowledge that I have cancer and the consequences of that for me and for all who love me and for my community.

With chemotherapy comes the hope of remission. What will I do with that if it comes? How long will it last? What is the most important goal for me if I do have a remission? And if I do not? And when, as is inevitable, the end does come, how do I face into that?

I woke up in the night last night worn out by anxiety, fear, resentment, unable to sleep, knowing I would begin chemotherapy in the morning. I sat before an icon, the Rublev "Holy Trinity" Jim McReynolds gave me when I was in the hospital, and prayed, *"Viens à mon aide, Seigneur"* over and over. It seemed to quiet and steady me a little. In my mind I had a strange companion whom I called Bojangles, a little creature made out of bones and vertebrae, tied together with ribbons, wearing a sly black hat, sitting there in his chair looking at me with glinting eyes, trying to get me. I called up "Imma," a veiled figure who comes up behind me, puts her hands on my shoulders, and defends me from Bojangles. I know these are creations of my own imagination, and I summoned them deliberately last night as I prayed, *"Viens à mon aide, Seigneur."*

If I ask myself, "What is most important thing to me now?" I answer, "The book, yes, but only if the book can be a catalyst for my community, for the healing of divisions." I looked again at the icon, and I focused on the cup of hospitality which is also the cup of sacrifice, acceptance of the stranger, seeing Christ in the other and in the enemy and in the opposition; seeing the face of God there. How do I do that? Unless I can do it, I do not suppose my words will empower anyone else. *"Seigneur, viens à mon aide."*

Last Sunday morning I started to read a medieval German dialogue with death called *The Plowman from Bohemia,* by Johannes von Saaz. As I was thinking about the meaning for me of healing and dying, my memory tells me how often I have healed before. Dying, of course, I cannot remember or recognize in my body; I can only understand it intellectually. I know I have ovarian cancer. I know cancer is a killer and that there is no known cure for it. I have agreed to chemotherapy which is not a cure, but a delayer. I read about the Plowman's defiance of death, his attacks on death, his rage, his philosophy, and I heard death reply with more philosophy. Where will the book end?

It ends, of course, with the voice of God, who takes over, and then with some moving prayers by the Plowman—the Plowman who plows with his pen. So I am here between healing and dying.

> Joy and rapture of the angels,
> molder of all highest forces,
> ancient of youthful days, hear me!

Since beginning this book, I have used the lucid weeks granted the patient in chemotherapy for writing, and now I am using the short lucid moments between heavy seda-

tion and the onset of fresh bouts of nausea and pain to finish the work. I want to end with the curious half-halluci-
nation and half-vision I had in the hospital after my first
operation. I saw a "river of blood" which was stormy, freely
rolling, filling the whole world. It was not a stream of
some red liquid, but a rollicking, serious, great flow of
creative love, the love of God for all creation. One could
just look and admire it; one could also, however, make the
deeply responsible commitment to it expressed by "turning." "Turn, turn, turn," says the prophet Amos—turn
from your wicked ways.

Turning to the stream of God's love is repentance—looking in a different direction, choosing to open oneself in repentance and sorrow in the cleansing stream. One could
go further if one chose; one could also join oneself, one's
life, with that stream, sharing in its power, which is power
for others.

> See where Christ's blood streams in the firmament....
> (Marlowe)

Appendix

Obedience & Community Responsibility

(Delivered at the Oxford Conference on Religious Life, 1965)

We are being asked to consider in this conference the relationship between Christians in religious communities and Christians in the world. We are to ask ourselves how far our rules and constitutions serve to foster a right relationship between the two groups. What should be the nature of our involvement in the powerful new movement in the Church and in the world today, and what adaptations in our government, in our community life, and the training of our novices and professed are needed if religious are to be taken seriously beyond the confines of their monastic establishments?

In this paper may we consider specifically the bearing of our formation in obedience upon our members and upon the corporate witness of our active and mixed communities in such areas as ecumenism, race relations and Christian citizenship.

1. Basis of obedience: two views

The Augustinian view is that "law is the expression of the all-holy essence and will of God engraved in the human heart *as appeal and invitation,* altogether personal and addressed to every man." Obedience, then, is a free and loving acceptance of the Word of God. The experience of obedience is an experience of illumination and of loving union with the will of God revealed as good. By obeying we share in the wisdom of God.

This concept of law is in opposition to the juridical positivism of the 19th century based on the false axiom: "God does not do anything because it is right. It is right because He commands it." Such a view of law produces in superiors mere domineering by means of orders "without furnishing insights and motivations. It breaks but does not educate." (Haring. *Law of Christ*, Vol. 1, 227.) In subjects it tends to destroy responsibility, and may result in neuroticism or rebellion. Neither does it permit the formation of a genuine corporate witness by a community because it substitutes exterior surrender for the interior consent necessary for a common mind.

Religious obedience is not essentially different from the obedience due to God speaking through authority in any walk of life. By the vow of obedience religious locate their obligation according to the rule and constitutions of their order.

2. Obedience and personal development.

There are two expressions used about obedience which are sources of confusion and dismay to many aspirants and novices. One is "blind obedience," and the other is "submission of judgment."

To speak of "blind obedience" is to speak of an imperfection, not an ideal. It is only because of the darkness sin causes in our minds that Christian obedience is ever blind. All men have sometimes to obey without knowing the reason why because of their limitations or their weaknesses. Perfect obedience, on the other hand, expands our hearts and enlightens our minds.

The expression "submission of judgment" is equally troublesome and misleading. It has also served as an invitation to caricature the religious life in several recent popular novels which have been widely and uncritically read.

Is a religious bound to agree with all her superiors? Must she believe the rule is infallible? Obviously not, for there could then be no point in constitutional provisions, for instance, for the deposition of a superior, or the amendment of the rule, and the safeguards of conscience would become inoperative.

According to the teaching of St. Thomas Aquinas, it is neither possible nor desirable to try to submit our speculative judgment to any creature. The speculative intellect is one of the highest powers of the soul, given us for the apprehension of necessary things, of first principles.

If a religious is required to carry out an order that seems to him unwise, he is bound to obey unless it would involve him directly in sin. He is *not* bound to break the links of a logical argument by force, or to pull his mind around so as to agree with his superior. To do so would be untruthful. God has given us minds to think with, and He does not wish us to use our wills for that purpose.

But he is to submit his practical judgment, an intellectual power which judges means or contingent things. This he can do by realising that God can work good through the authorities He sanctions and sustains, even when they are mistaken. It will help to perfect his obedience if he also considers that he himself may be the mistaken one, and that a superior may have access to facts unknown to him, wider experience and a broader view. He cannot rightly, however, abandon ideas which seem right to him, nor bid his conscience assess a course of action as desirable simply because it is commanded.

The donation of self through the vows involves sacrifice and loss. Many possibilities must go unrealized and many latent powers undeveloped. The negative aspect of the vow of obedience is important. It may cost us all we are capable of giving to keep that vow. This is often borne in upon us in our spiritual reading and in retreat addresses, under the images of darkness and death. It would be dangerous to neglect this side of the truth.

There is, however, the other aspect, the positive one. Self is not a pure evil. It is a creature of God of a very high order and it must be rightly loved and valued. Obedience is not confined to not doing things. It sets us free to use our powers of mind and will to the utmost of our capacity. Religious orders should be fostering by every means the personal growth of its members. Some of these means are: an atmosphere of warmth and encouragement, sensitiveness to the needs of others at times for privacy and at times for support and understanding. The possibility of legitmate emotional satisfaction in friendship, in significant work for others, and in creating things which are beautiful and useful. The self which is offered to God in obedience must be integrated and developed, capable of autonomous acts. We must give God our human best.

All this is not to say that the spirit of man is dependent upon means or circumstances for holiness. The martyrology teaches us otherwise. So do the letters from prison written by victims in the German concentration camps of World War 2. Solitary confinement, degrading and brutalising treatment, terror and pain and the threat of death sometimes brought out the best and purest in man. (It might make the martyrology more relevant is we included in it some of these witnesses, Protestant and Jewish as well as Catholic.)

No one would argue from this that concentration camps are good patterns for Christian Societies! God has designed a sacramental world, and has set men in families under the law of love. The new Commandment, that we should love one another as He loves, should be the inspiration of every religious custom and rule.

A mistaken view of obedience can have grave consequences for individual religious. To subject a person to moral pressure based upon power tends to produce a neurotic, a hypocrite or a rebel. Each member of Chapter bears the burden of guilt for the harm the community does by a false view of authority. Our rules should allow members legitimate expression of conscience in this matter, an opportunity to discuss their concerns with other members of Chapter, and to recommend measures for reform. Nor must they be cut off from guidance from discreet and qualified persons outside the community when they feel the need for it.

3. Obedience and corporate witness.

When we consider the meaning of our communities for those outside them, our bearing upon the larger community in which we live and to which we witness by our lives as well as by our works, we see the same need, in corporate form, for intelligent and responsible action. If we are to have anything to say as communities to the world without, we must have among ourselves an openness of mind that encourages the honest appraisal of new ideas. We must have the habit of sharing our difficulties and our insights with one another, and an atmosphere of freedom in discussion. We must have access to pertinent information and an adequate preparation, both remote and proximate, for our work.

By "remote" I mean the general theological, liturgical and professional formation which an order gives its members. Unless we are constantly receptive to new ideas, willing to give a hearing even to the most disturbing, we run the risk of becoming what someone has called "Anglo-Catholic ghettoes," unable to talk to anyone except other Anglo-Catholics. Our libraries should contain up-to-date biblical and theological studies, controversial and current books which serious people are reading today, and books written from points of view other than our own. It is not enough to read such books with an eye to refuting them. Conceivably they may have something to say to us and we may miss it if we read in too defensive or hostile a spirit.

An example of "proximate" preparation is the specific training for foreign service which should be undertaken by communities with missions abroad. This should include cultural anthropology, linguistics and a study of the literature and history, political, social and economic of the country to which religious are sent. Missionaries can no longer go out to the undeveloped countries with the idea of bringing enlightenment to those in darkness. They must go out to seek and find Christ in men and women of other cultures and to become partners with them in the common worship and work of the Church in their land.

The same principles apply to active work at home. Without an open-minded and informed approach, our teaching, counselling and social work will become more and more irrelevant, and we shall find ourselves ministering only to the already persuaded.

If our communities are to have anything to say in response to the urgencies of today, ecumenism, race relations, missionary strategy, questions about marriage and sex, social questions in many areas, we must have not only informed individuals according to their capacities, but informed societies. A mechanical view of obedience hampers and sometimes entirely discourages independent thinking, and the best is needed from everyone. The wrong application of authority, perhaps in the form of a demand for submission of judgment may serve to blind whole communities to objective justice and make reform and renewal impossible. Group planning and evaluation are necessary if religious orders are to make a genuine corporate witness. The effort to form a common mind is a costing one and may not always be successful. There must be an honorable place for a conscientious minority. A common mind, however, is worth waiting for as long as possible. From it alone can a community speak from the depths of its corporate worship and fraternal love.

Religious obedience in its highest form is the enlightened act of mind and will whereby a subject lays hold on the vision of goodness and right which God gives to a superior. It makes possible the genuine growth towards God of both superior and subject. Through its operation in mutual love and respect, it makes it possible also for the community to receive and be enlarged by the vision of goodness and right which God may give to the youngest of subjects. It thus serves to create a new and concrete expression of God's will upon earth and furthers His kingdom.

*C*owley Publications is a ministry of the Society of St. John the Evangelist, a religious community for men in the Episcopal Church. Emerging from the Society's tradition of prayer, theological reflection, and diversity of mission, the press is centered in the rich heritage of the Anglican Communion.

Cowley Publications seeks to provide books, audio cassettes, and other resources for the ongoing theological exploration and spiritual development of the Episcopal Church and others in the body of Christ. To this end, it is dedicated to developing a new generation of theological writers, encouraging them to produce timely, creative, and stimulating publications of excellence, and making these publications available widely, reaching both clergy and lay persons.